LAWNS
AND
LANDSCAPING

LAWNS
AND
LANDSCAPING

1001 Gardening Questions Answered

by

The Editors of Garden Way Publishing

Foreword by Bob Thomson

A GARDEN WAY PUBLISHING BOOK

STOREY COMMUNICATIONS, INC.
POWNAL, VERMONT 05261

Produced by Storey Communications, Inc.
President, M. John Storey
Executive Vice President of Administration, Martha M. Storey
Executive Vice President of Operations, Douglas B. Rhodes
Publisher, Thomas Woll

Written by Roger M. Griffith and the Editors of Garden Way
    Publishing
Cover and text design by Andrea Gray
Edited by Gwen W. Steege
Production by Andrea Gray and Rebecca Babbitt
Front cover photograph by A. Blake Gardner
Back cover photograph by Gary Mottau, Positive Images
Interior photographs by Walter Chandoha, A. Blake Gardner, New
    York Turfgrass, Maggie Oster, Positive Images (Tad Goodale,
    Margaret Hensel, Jerry Howard, Gary Mottau), Ann Reilly, Ringer
    Corporation
Chapter opening photographs: 1, A. Blake Gardner; 2, Positive
    Images, Jerry Howard; 3, 4, and 6, Positive Images, Gary Mottau;
    5, Maggie Oster
Drawings by Alison Kolesar and Wanda Harper
Map by Northern Cartographic
Typesetting by The Best Type & Design on Earth, Burlington, VT

Copyright © 1989 by Doubleday Book & Music Clubs, Inc.

Library of Congress Catalog Card Number: 88-45619
International Standard Book Number: 0-88266-535-9 (hardcover)

Library of Congress Cataloging-in-Publication Data

Lawns and landscaping— ; 1,001 gardening questions
    answered.

    Bibliography: p.
    Includes index.
    1. Landscape gardening—Miscellanea. 2. Lawns—Miscel-
lanea. I. Garden Way Publishing.
SB473.L39   1989   635.9   88-45619
ISBN 0-88266-535-9

Contents

Lawns and Landscaping is a reference book, crammed full of basic information designed to equip increasingly discerning and eager gardeners for their lawn and landscaping tasks. From the time of the first mechanical lawn mower in England in 1830, until after World War II, when lawn care became a serious matter for those living in the rapidly expanding suburban areas, lawn and landscaping techniques have become more and more sophisticated. Until fairly recently, however, questions that arose frequently went unanswered. Garden centers were almost nonexistent a few decades ago, and agricultural county extension agents were busy with the commercial side of horticulture, with little time for answering the myriad questions posed by a growing multitude of suburbanites. Gardeners were forced to seek information from nurseries and hardware and farm supply stores with garden departments, the forerunners of the garden center industry as we know it today. Even now, those who wish to do their own lawn and landscaping work, to save money or simply to exercise their own creativity, may find it difficult to find accurate, practical information. For this reason alone, *Lawns and Landscaping* is worthy of a prominent position on the book shelf of any person who is inclined to do even a minimal amount of lawn work or landscaping.

Let me give you some examples of what you can expect when you use this book as a ready reference. In the lawn section, for example, you will find information on building a new lawn and renovating an old one. You will learn how to select the proper grass seed mixture for your area of the country; what fertilizer is best and when to apply it; why and how you should apply lime; when to water an established lawn; how to control insect and disease problems; and how to grow an all-organic lawn.

The landscape section suggests how to plan your own landscaping, with advice on how to draw a relatively simple landscape plan showing the existing features and topography that must be integrated into the ultimate design. Equally important are the sections on choosing and planting the right plants, trees, and shrubs for your own situation, using flowers in the landscape, and incorporating walls, walks, pathways, and patios into your design.

The concluding chapter is likely to be a special favorite, with lively ideas about creating kitchen, herb, and rock gardens, and gardens for the elderly, or perhaps handicapped, persons. There are also tips on gardening with children and attracting birds to your garden.

If you have a problem with your lawn or landscape, you can be sure that others have had similar problems, and all those problems—and their solutions—are now organized and indexed in this book, ready and waiting for you, the reader, to turn the pages. And by the way, if you conscientiously follow the advice given herewith, you will find that your landscape efforts will pay substantial dividends during the years ahead. Your property will increase in value, you will have created a private, practical, and peaceful haven for you and your family, and you will have achieved a quality of life that exceeds your present expectations.

Bob Thomson, Master Gardener
Host of "The Victory Garden," PBS

LAWNS
AND
LANDSCAPING

1 Creating a New Lawn or Rebuilding an Old One

For all those who are fortunate enough to have some open space around the place where they live, a lawn, no matter how modest, can be a source of pleasure and pride. It can also be a challenge, evoking a thousand and one questions related to its creation and maintenance. In the pages that follow, you will find the answers to many of those questions, so that you can approach your lawnkeeping tasks with a new understanding of grass's growing habits and needs. The ideal—a healthy, lush carpet of green—is within the reach of anyone who wishes it, and with less difficulty than you might think.

Today, a "good" lawn consists of an overcrowded population of dwarf grass plants—often a thousand or more shoots to the square foot—all so very much alike as to create an unblemished surface, a carpetlike lawn. This provides a superlative backdrop for home landscaping, whether the emphasis is on flower gardens or the form and texture effects created by trees, shrubs, and the varied grasses themselves. We expect this dense, perpetually defoliated carpet to be constantly solid underfoot, so that pets and people walking over it are well out of the mud in all seasons. It must look good even when given inexpert attention, refresh the air, cool the environs in summer, insulate the ground in winter, prevent soil erosion, sometimes even serve as a playfield and a picnic ground. The grass family alone provides the qualities that meet all these requirements.

There are several approaches to acquiring this kind of lush carpet in your front and backyards, and what approach you take depends on what you have to start with, how much you are interested in doing yourself, and the amount you are willing to

◀ *A carpetlike lawn provides a superlative backdrop for home landscaping.*

1

spend to achieve the desired results. If you have just built a new home, creating a lawn from the raw earth is a big undertaking, requiring rototilling and grading to do the job right. You may decide to hire someone else to do these chores if your area is large. For small lawns, you can do the tilling yourself with a rented or purchased rotary tiller and the grading with a steel garden rake, or better still a landscaping rake. In the pages that follow you will find step-by-step instructions on how to proceed, so that even if you decide to contract out some or all of the work, you will find here valuable information on how to give your lawn a good healthy beginning, thus saving disappointment and added work in years to come.

Those who have established lawns with bare spots, weeds, drainage problems, or the host of other difficulties that plague lawnkeepers, will find suggestions on how to correct and avoid these flaws, and even information on how to rebuild the lawn completely—again a big project requiring a commitment of time and energy.

Whether your tasks are major or minor, they are doable, and the results will make you glad you made the effort. Let's begin with creating an entirely new lawn.

PREPARING THE SITE

The first and most urgent consideration when developing a lawn is to improve the soil *before* spreading the seed. There are many kinds of lawn grasses (see pages 12–13), and most are widely adaptable. They will grow in soils having a range of nutrient content (*fertility*; see pages 30–34), with wide pH dif-

Ringer Corporation

The ideal lawn consists of an overcrowded population of dwarf grass plants. This unblemished surface is constantly solid underfoot, cools and freshens the air in summer, insulates in winter, and prevents soil erosion. Here, the lawn is Kentucky bluegrass.

THE EVOLUTION OF LAWNS

Centuries ago, lawns were "mowed" by the livestock that, for their safety, grazed near their owner's homes. The advantages of having lawns were so obvious that by the Middle Ages wide swards were kept within bounds by scything.

The first mechanical lawn mower was invented in 1830 in England. About a century later, gasoline-propelled mowers were common, and soon these conveniences had changed the face of American towns. While in years past, well-tended lawns, blemished by neither dandelion nor crabgrass, were seen only around the mansions of the rich, by World War II carefully tended lawns—lawns that were fed, weeded, mowed, and watered— became the rule. The days of merely trimming whatever vegetation volunteered were over, even for those of more modest means. Ultimately, small tractors with grass-clipping blades spinning beneath rolled onto the scene, providing country towns and suburbs alike with acres of carpetlike lawns.

ferences (*acidity*; see page 34–36), and varying from clayey to sandy (*texture*; see page 6). You will have a healthier, more carefree lawn, however, if the soil's fertility, acidity, and texture are optimal. The ideal soil for a healthy lawn is three to five inches of good *loam* (soil that is neither very sandy nor very clayey), rich in organic matter. Once a lawn is established, fertilizers and other soil treatments can be applied only at ground surface rather than around the grasses' roots where they are most beneficial. The extra efforts you make to be certain your soil is of top quality before you grade, roll, and seed your new lawn, therefore, will pay gratifying dividends in years ahead.

When should I sow my new lawn?

It depends entirely on where you live. Here are a few general rules to guide you, but you might want to check with your Extension Service agent for the best advice for your particular area. In the South, the grasses that grow most rapidly in the heat are best started in the spring, whether you decide to use grass seed or to put down sod. In the central area of the country, from Philadelphia and Washington, D.C., west to the Plains, fall seeding is recommended. In the more northern areas, seeding is possible in both spring and fall, though fall is recommended, because the cool nights and fall rains encourage grass growth and make frequent watering less necessary. Also, early frosts tend to kill weeds before they can go to seed and spread through the lawn. In the Western Plains, seeding should be done in the spring to take advantage of the period of greatest rainfall during the summer months.

What time of year is best for starting a lawn in southern California?

A lawn may be started at any time, but the best time is in the early fall—September or October. The plants will be well established before winter's heavy rains, and a good turf should be underway before summer's heat.

I'm planning to start a lawn. Any hints before I sow the grass seed?

Grade the soil so any water will drain away from the house. Don't leave any low spots that will turn into puddles after every rain. You can check for low spots by running a taut string between two stakes so that the string just touches the ground. You will be able to see immediately any areas that fall below the level of the string. Also, rake the finished soil surface so that it is one or two inches below the level of walks and driveways; this will save you hours of edging in future summers and look far neater.

A string stretched taut between two stakes reveals low areas in the seedbed that will cause puddling in the lawn if not corrected.

How much grade must be given a new lawn, and how is the grade determined?

A grade of one foot in twenty, or even thirty, feet is sufficient to give surface drainage. The grade can be established by using a line level, but in most cases simple sighting can assure you that the slope will provide adequate drainage away from the house. When you water the area, note runoff and any areas of ponding.

How would you grade the front lawn of a small house that is several feet below the highway level?

A gradual slope from the house up to the street is more pleasing than an abrupt terrace. To prevent water from draining into the house, however, the grade should first be carried down

In order to prevent drainage problems, maintain a grade away from the house of 1 foot for every 20 feet.

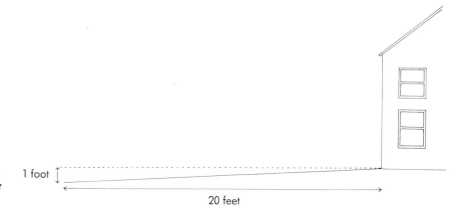

1 foot

20 feet

STEPS IN PREPARING THE SITE FOR A NEW LAWN

- Remove all building debris and large stones from the site. Bottles, cans, bricks, and wood waste will obstruct roots, impede water movement, and sometimes cause disease. Mushrooms, not welcome in lawns, are the fruiting bodies of fungi living on rotting wood in the soil.

If you decide to add topsoil, first grade the area, to make certain drainage will be carried away from the house and to avoid small hills and valleys in the lawn that are both unsightly and a source of puddling. Use a steel garden rake or arrange for mechanical equipment if the work entails moving a lot of soil. Steep slopes should be terraced rather than graded; although grasses will grow on steep slopes, mowing will be a headache. If you plan to use a riding mower, it is particularly important to determine the slope that the mower will navigate safely. Remember, you are actually creating a subgrade on which you will be adding topsoil; keep the top of this subgrade four to eight inches below the desired finished lawn level.

This area is being graded prior to addition of topsoil, which will be trucked in. Dotted line shows finished lawn level, 4 to 6 inches above subgrade.

the subsoil using a rotary power tiller, if necessary. Chopped hay, leaves, rotted sawdust, rotted manure, compost, and peat are all effective for this purpose. A one- to three-inch-deep layer is acceptable and more is helpful. Add 50 to 100 pounds of lime and 10 to 15 pounds of superphosphate per 1,000 square feet. Mix all of this into the subsoil with a tiller or by hand.

- Add a layer of topsoil, three to five inches in depth. Figure on twelve cubic yards per 1,000 square feet of lawn. Ideally, this topsoil should be tested, using a soil-testing kit available from garden centers or by sending soil samples to your Extension Service. Chemical fertilizers should then be added and tilled in if needed.

Positive Images, Jerry Howard

After watering or heavy rains, puddled areas quickly indicate trouble spots where grading must be improved.

- Maintain the existing grade around trees. Lowering the grade may damage tree roots; raising it will change the amount of oxygen available to them from the soil. Many trees will tolerate up to eight inches of additional soil, or fill; some, such as oaks, are threatened by two or three additional inches. To avoid this threat, build a rockwell, extending out three or more feet all around the tree.

- Before adding the topsoil, mix organic matter into

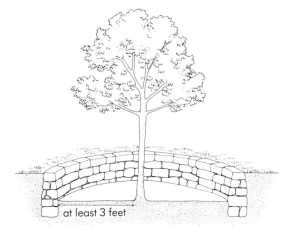

When grading results in a ground level too high for existing trees, construct a retaining wall (called a rockwell) at least 3 feet from the tree trunk, so that roots maintain their original level and thus receive adequate air and moisture.

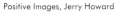

from the house slightly, to a low point from which the water can drain off to the sides before the slope up to the street begins.

Our backyard has no flat areas to use for a patio or play area. Could I terrace it?

Terracing can be very effective in such a situation. If the area is large, you may need to hire someone to do the work of pushing the earth into two or more flat levels that will be held in place by retaining walls of such materials as stone or railroad ties.

If there is much unevenness in the ground, should it be dug or plowed before being graded?

The soil, of course, will have to be loosened to move it. Although it is a lot of work, the practical thing to do is to remove all the topsoil, loosen and enrich the often more compacted and less fertile subsoil, grade the area and then finish the grade with the topsoil. This ensures an even depth of good soil over the entire area.

I know that the type of soil is important when starting a lawn, but how can I determine what kind of soil I have? Mine looks like a mixture of clay and sand—with some gravel.

Put a cup of your soil into a quart jar. Add a cup of water. Screw on the top and swirl the mixture. Let it settle, and repeat this procedure several times. Now allow the mixture to stand until the water is clear. The various-sized particles will settle out in layers with the clay on top and the larger ones—sand—below it. If the top layer is deepest, you have clay soil; if the bottom one is deepest, you have sandy soil. If the various layers are fairly equal, consider yourself lucky because you have a balanced soil.

Soils are generally broken down into three groups—*sandy soils*, *loamy soils*, and *clayey soils*.

Sandy soils range from very fine sands, with 50 percent or more of very fine sands, to coarse sands containing 35 percent or more of fine gravel and less than 50 percent finer sands. Any of these soils will form into a ball when moist, but the ball will break easily when touched.

Loamy soils have about a 50-50 mixture of sand and silt-clay. A ball of damp, loamy soil will not break when handled.

Clayey soils range from those containing 30-percent clay to those that are nearly 100-percent clay. Clay is fine-textured and sticky when wet.

The varieties of grass seed you can grow successfully and the type and amount of lawn care you must do are determined in part by the kind of soil you have.

Can thin soils and stony ground be used to start a new lawn?

These are trouble areas. If there is sufficient soil to support grass roots and the drainage is adequate, a stony soil can be

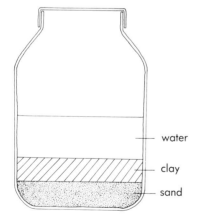

water

clay

sand

To determine what type soil you have, place 1 cup of soil in a quart jar with 1 cup of water. Shake and allow the mixture to settle several times and then note the relative size of sand and clay layers. The soil illustrated is a fairly balanced one, with clay and sand layers about equal.

made into a good lawn. Even so, any obtrusive stones that materially interfere either with the level of the land or the use of a mower should be removed. Rocky outcrops are very difficult, for they tend to hold moisture in rainy periods and to dry out quickly during dry weather. You have two choices in such instances. One is to bring in enough good soil to provide at least four inches of rooting area over the poor base. The other is to forget about a lawn and treat the area as a semirock garden with appropriate plantings (see pages 131–33).

The area where we hope to create a lawn is heavy clay. One of my neighbors tells me to add lots of sand to improve it; another one tells me to add organic matter. Which one is right?

Sand alone will not do too much to improve the soil; in fact, it may even "set up" in the clay as it does in concrete. You can add some sand, but concentrate instead on incorporating as much organic material as you can. Loosen the compacted soil at least two or three inches deep by tilling and then add six or more inches of organic material, such as compost, rotted manure, or peat moss, to help lighten the heavy soil. You can then work in it earlier in the spring. Organic material also permits better aeration around the roots and adds nutrients to the soil. Sand does none of these. Ideally, you would make this a continuing project, adding more organic material each year, but because you are seeding the area for a lawn, you must make your addition to the clay a heavy one: You will not be able to till lawn areas up regularly to work on soil texture improvement. In the worst cases, you may decide to remove some of the clay and replace it with good topsoil.

Heavy soils are not completely bad. They have the advantage of holding moisture and soil nutrients relatively well.

Why shouldn't clay be worked when wet?

Clay compacts easily, especially when wet. It then puddles and hardens, making it practically useless for at least one growing season. Clay is made up of the tiniest particles—1,000 or more of them together are the size of a single particle of sand. When damp, a handful of clay will form a very slick, pliable ball. As it dries, it becomes hard, with a baked appearance. For instance, air circulating around the surfaces of the fist-sized chunks kicked up by a tiller causes them to dry and harden quickly, leaving a garden in which it is impossible to get seeds to germinate and grow. Clay, the last of the soil to dry in the spring, should not, therefore, be worked when it is wet. If you have a clay soil, learn to judge when the soil can be worked: It is impossible when puddles can be seen. After the water slowly penetrates the soil, step on it, then look at the footprint. If it is shiny, wait before tilling. The only long-term solution for the inconvenience of having to wait to work this soil at the proper time is to add organic matter to it, year after year. This will separate that mass of tiny particles and provide space in the soil so both air and moisture can move through it.

My tract of land has a heavy, tough, red clay base, with only a light topsoil covering. What is the best treatment?

In the spring, grow a cover crop of soybeans and till them in before the beans are ripe. Follow with a crop of rye, leave it in place over the winter, and till it under the next spring.

What about planting a lawn on sandy soil?

Sandy soils have the advantage of not compacting easily and needing little cultivation. On the other hand, they do not hold moisture or fertilizer nutrients well. To offset this problem, mix in at least an inch of organic material, such as peat moss or weed-free compost (see page 107) when preparing the soil for planting. Even without special modifications, a sandy soil can be made to support grass if fertilized and watered lightly and frequently.

We are ready to build a new house on a lot and wonder if we should plan our lawn now?

You can plan it, but wait until the house is built before actually planting a lawn. The most important thing to do initially is to plan the lawn's location. Before your cellar hole is dug, have the contractor scrape away all of the topsoil where both the house and the lawn will be, and set it aside. The cellar hole earth can then be spread over the entire site and the topsoil distributed on top, saving you the expense of buying and trucking in topsoil for the lawn. Alternatively, you may prefer simply to have the cellar hole subsoil hauled away.

Is bringing in topsoil advisable when starting a new lawn?

This depends on how adequate your soil is. If the soil is very thin, topsoil may be needed. But in many instances, the residual soil can be improved sufficiently to make a good seedbed for much less than additional topsoil would cost. Moreover, topsoil is often of poor quality, not necessarily fertile, and almost invariably full of weed seeds.

If, in starting a lawn, I truck in topsoil, should I add fertilizer to it?

There is no way to know whether, or how much, to fertilize without having the soil tested (see pages 30–36). Usually, however, people want to spread the topsoil and seed it immediately. If you must do this, it's good to add ground limestone (unless you live in an area where you know soils are generally alkaline) and a complete garden fertilizer to the soil. Using a fertilizer spreader, broadcast fifty pounds of ground limestone per 1,000 square feet, using dolomitic limestone with magnesium, if it is available at your garden center. Fertilize sandy topsoils with thirty pounds of 5-10-10 or fifteen pounds of 10-20-20. Clays and loams require thirty pounds of 5-10-5 or fifteen pounds of 10-20-10. Don't use so-called special lawn fertilizers before seeding a lawn. They do not add enough phosphorus or potassium for establishment.

If you prefer using organic materials, apply limestone as above and substitute fifty pounds of rock phosphate plus 500 pounds of rotted cow manure for the commercial fertilizer.

Work both commercial and organic fertilizers into the soil with a rake or, better, by tilling.

I expect to purchase topsoil for my lawn site. How will it be dumped on my lot?

You control this. Most drivers will run the soil off the truck so that it is spread roughly where it should be. Others will spot loads where the soil is needed. Then you can complete the spreading. For this, use a steel garden rake or a landscaping rake, which is three or four feet in width, with large teeth to catch the soil. This rake simplifies the task and makes getting a good grade much easier. To prevent unnecessary compaction of the soil, do not allow trucks to drive over the ground any more than absolutely necessary.

I'm planning to improve the sandy soil around my house by adding a lot of topsoil. How much should I add?

To get the most value out of added topsoil, first work as much organic matter as you can into the soil already on the site. This can be leaves, hay, peat moss, or material from a partially decomposed compost pile. This material will help to hold moisture and prevent the topsoil you spread from being washed down through the sand. Next, add about three inches of topsoil, and till or spade it to a depth of six inches. Complete the job by working fertilizer, either commercial or decayed manure, into the soil. Your soil is now ready for a lawn (or a garden).

How high can the soil be raised around a tree without injuring it?

This varies with the kind of tree, the soil, and the effectiveness of surface drainage. In general, where the soil is light and well drained, the grade may be raised around trees eight inches without appreciable injury. If the soil is heavy and poorly drained, raising the grade as little as two or three inches may cause waterlogging and make it impossible for necessary oxygen to reach the tree roots (see also page 5).

How thoroughly should the soil be cultivated before sowing?

Seedbed cultivation has these objectives: to break up any clods; to destroy unwanted vegetation; to mix fertilizer into the

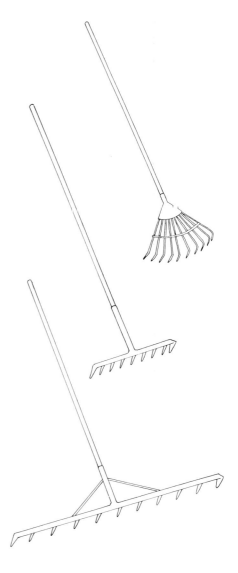

From top: leaf rake, garden rake, landscaping rake.

soil; to loosen the soil enough so that air exchange occurs well beneath the surface, permitting deeper root growth; and to create a pebbled surface that accepts seed well and allows water to penetrate. Overtilling is possible. It will pulverize the soil past the pebbled surface stage desired, eliminating the larger pieces that are so helpful for the movement of air and water into the soil.

Must the soil for a lawn be fertilized?

Most soils benefit from fertilization. To determine the fertility levels, use a soil-testing kit or send a soil sample to your Extension Service and follow the recommendations suggested by the results. If the addition of phosphorus is recommended, now is the time to add it. Phosphorus tends to stay at the level where it is applied, unlike other nutrients that leach down into the soil. Thus, if applied after the lawn is planted, it remains near the surface, out of reach of the roots.

Should I roll the lawn area before seeding it?

Yes, but do not overdo it. First, rake the area, breaking up any surface crust. It's good to rake in both directions, to get the proper grade for the lawn. Then roll the area with a lawn roller, and rake again in both directions. This gives a fairly compact surface, but with a pebbled top into which seeds will drop. The surface is good when it shows only a very shallow footprint when you walk on it. If the soil is quite sandy, don't worry about overcompacting it—you can't.

A well-prepared seedbed offers a rough, pebbled surface for seeds and is firm enough to show only a shallow footprint.

CHOOSING THE RIGHT SEED

Because of the many fine turf species for lawns, there are some for almost any geographical area and every soil, shade, or moisture condition. The number grows as new cultivars are offered each year. While most grass species are started from seed, many are propagated in other ways. Some have surface runners, called *stolons*. Others have underground spreading stems, called *rhizomes*. Stolons, *sprigs* (young shoots), or *plugs* (small cubes of sod) are often used to start lawns.

Some grasses have a greater tendency than others to create *thatch*, a layer of dead grass that builds up between the soil and the grass blades, and cuts off the flow of moisture down to the roots.

How do I know which package of seed mixture to choose?

There is, or course, no limit to the grass seed mixtures that can be offered. Study the accompanying Extension Service list, which demonstrates how mixture can be created for specific conditions.

Why are mixtures of grass seed offered?

Seed dealers package mixtures in an effort to introduce enough variability into the lawn so that not all the grass will be susceptible to the same affliction. Because of the necessary overcrowding of the grass plants that make up a lawn, individual plants are apt to be weaker than they might be if uncrowded and unmowed. If all were hereditarily alike, they would be fair game for diseases, which, if they encounter no resistance readily spread from one plant to another. When grass blends or mixtures are used, some resistant grass may confront whatever disease or other pest invades the lawn. One cultivar, or variety, may suffer in an attack by a certain disease, while another grass remains resistant.

In addition, some grasses are better suited than others to various conditions, such as sun and shade, south and north slopes, poor and good soil pockets. While a single cultivar would not adapt to all of these conditions, a mixture offers a range of possibilities. A bluegrass-fescue combination, with a bit of perennial ryegrass for quick cover, is a typical mixture. The bluegrasses are great for open areas, but the fescues will survive better in the shade and on dry, infertile soil under trees. Even when an all-bluegrass lawn is desirable, blends of cultivars are advocated to spread the risk.

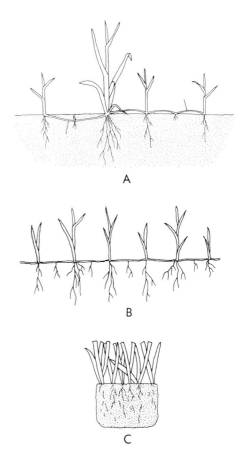

(A) Grass plants spread by surface runners, called stolons, and underground spreading stems, called rhizomes; (B) sprigs are stem fragments with young blades of grass and bits of root attached; (C) plugs are small cubes of sod, about 2 inches wide and 2 inches deep.

Seed Mixtures

SITUATION	KENTUCKY BLUEGRASS	CREEPING RED FESCUE	WINTER-HARDY RYEGRASS
General use in a diversity of situations and soils	20	40	40
Full sun, good fertility and management	50	20	30
Quick cover, but persistent	20	20	60
Clay soil, full sun, densely growing sod	100	—	—
Putting-green turf, to be mowed short	100[a]	—	—
Slope, never to be mowed	20	60	20
Temporary cover for summer	—	—	100 (annual)
Dry, sandy soils, open shade, or under trees	20[b]	80	—
Moist shade much of day, under trees, or north side of house	30[b]	40	30

a Use low-growing varieties, such as Glade and Nugget.
b Use shade-tolerant varieties, such as A-34, Nugget, Glade, and Touchdown.

Seed mixtures combine such variants as shade- and sun-loving grasses so that the lawn is adaptable to different conditions.

Do you have any comments on buying grass seed?

Just one piece of advice: Read the label. Most states now require the labeling of grass seed containers to show the species, variety, purity, weed seed content, and germination. The seed must be laboratory tested within the current year. Seeds should have at least 75- to 80-percent germination and 85- to 90-percent purity. The higher the content of pure live seeds, the less seed you need to sow. If you have some seed left over after sowing, save it. You'll find a use for it: Seeds are good for up to three years if stored in a cool, dry place. Freezing won't hurt them if they are kept dry.

There are so many new grass varieties (cultivars) now. How can I choose intelligently?

It is helpful to realize that all bluegrasses behave somewhat alike, and the same is true with other varieties. The difference between individual cultivars is mostly a matter of preferred color, texture, or growth habit. Care is less of a consideration. Seed firms provide helpful information about their own cultivars, and responsible houses will utilize quality components in their seed mixtures that you can accept on faith. The new cultivars would not have been brought to market had they not exhibited at least some superior characteristics. They are chosen for reasonable resistance to the usual lawn diseases, for comparatively low rather than tall growth, and for their attractive appearance.

SOUTHERN TURF SPECIES

Typically planted from Tennessee southward, these grasses grow best at relatively warm temperatures (above 80° F.). They experience most growth in spring and summer and should therefore receive major attention then.

BAHIA GRASS, *Paspalum notatum*. This fairly open, coarse grass has unattractive seed heads and is hard to mow. It is one of the easiest southern turf grasses to plant and to care for, however, and is sometimes used in mixtures.

BERMUDA GRASS, *Cynodon Dactylon* and hybrids. Bermuda grass has an attractive texture and deep color if well tended. Fast-growing and aggressive, it is so vigorous that it requires frequent mowing. It is a pest in flower and shrub beds and readily forms thatch. It grows in sun only, ceases growth when

temperatures fall and is doubtfully hardy north of Tennessee.

CENTIPEDE GRASS, *Eremochloa ophiuroides*. This medium-textured, low-maintenance grass actually suffers if fertilized too heavily, but it does need iron. It turns yellowish unless soils are acid.

ST. AUGUSTINE GRASS, *Stenotaphrum secundatum*. St. Augustine grass is coarse but not unattractive. Its few seed heads are usually dark green. This grass is subject to chinch bug and several diseases, but resistant cultivars can be purchased. It tends to form thatch and is tolerant of shade.

ZOYSIA GRASS, *Zoysia Matrella*. Slow-growing, dense, and attractive, zoysia grass does not require a great deal of attention. It is very fibrous and tough to mow. Billbug damage can be serious.

NORTHERN TURF SPECIES

These grasses grow best when temperatures do not exceed 80° F. (at least at night). They conserve resources best in autumn, winter, and spring, are weakest in summer, and benefit most from attention in autumn.

BENT GRASS, *Agrostis*. Bent grass has small light green to blue-green leaf blades with excellent texture. Low, trailing, or semitrailing, bent grass spreads by above-ground stolons. Like other trailing stoloniferous grasses, it tends to build up a mat of vegetation on the soil surface. If this is slow to decompose, it will quickly create a layer of interfering thatch. It is a fine "show" grass for turfs that are fertilized, watered, and frequently mowed, but it is prone to diseases in muggy weather and to snow-mold under cool, damp conditions. It is used on greens at golf courses and is not commonly chosen for home lawns.

New York Turfgrass

The lower half of this illustration is a weed, an annual bluegrass in full seedhead stage. The upper half shows good Kentucky bluegrass.

KENTUCKY BLUEGRASS, *Poa pratensis*. This deep green grass has gracefully arching shoots and fine- to medium-textured, uniform foliage. Spread by rhizomes, it forms one of the thickest and most vigorous sods, well able to compete with weeds. Widely adaptable, it is one of the best all-around grasses and rather easy to care for.

FINE FESCUE, *Festuca rubra* in varieties. Also known as red fescue, this attractively fine-textured, beautifully dark green grass is rather stiff, with a windswept appearance. Best in cooler seasons, it may become patchy under hot and humid conditions. One of the finest shade grasses, it persists on poorish soils in dry locations. Because it wears well, it makes an excellent playing surface.

New York Turfgrass

Some grass species have desirable forms as well as those of lesser quality. Tall fescue is here contrasted with the more desirable fine, turf-type fescue.

TALL FESCUE, *Festuca elatior*. A tall grass, common in meadows and pastures, but four varieties, while coarser than Kentucky bluegrass, are drought-tolerant and satisfactory for lawns. Both fine and tall fescue produce rhizomes.

PERENNIAL RYEGRASS, *Lolium perenne*. The new turf types of ryegrass bred for lawns are just as attractive as bluegrass. Their shiny green leaves are quick to sprout, grow rapidly, and are tough. They adapt to a wide range of soil types, form a thick cover, and are easy to maintain. Ryegrass is reasonably hardy, although not so widely adapted to climatic extremes as Kentucky bluegrass. Because ryegrass does not spread and the seeds are larger than other grass seeds, it must be sown more densely than any other grass, about six pounds or more per 1,000 square feet.

How can I avoid confusing good lawn grasses with poor ones?

Unfortunately, some uncertainty occurs with common names, and the botanical names seldom appear on the packages, or, if they do, they are easily misunderstood by the uninitiated. As an example, "bluegrass" generally refers to the valuable Kentucky bluegrass species, *Poa pratensis*. Note, however: "Annual" bluegrass is a weed, and other bluegrasses, such as Canada or Woods, are of lesser quality. To add confusion, Kentucky-31 is a tall fescue (*Festuca elatior*) with coarse blades, and is definitely not a Kentucky bluegrass. It is easy to be misled, and it pays to acquaint yourself with lawn grasses in order to recognize their names on the required seed package list.

I don't want to make a lifetime mission out of caring for the lawn I am planning, but it is a fairly large lawn. Any ideas on what I should plant?

Look for some of the old-fashioned, self-reliant cultivars so well adapted to the casual care of yesteryear. Among the Kentucky bluegrasses are Arboretum (Missouri) and Kenblue (Kentucky) strains for the southern portions of the bluegrass belt, and Park (Minnesota) for northern and western zones. They are best mowed fairly tall, with at least a two-inch clipping height (see page 38). Some of the newer cultivars, such as Birka and Plush, are similar. Also, the better recent cultivars, such as Rugby, Parade, and Baron, while they are finest when well cared for, do reasonably well under some neglect.

What is meant by nurse grass?

This term is not common anymore, since the methods of starting a lawn have changed. In older seed mixtures, nurse grass was the grass that came up first, until the slower starting, permanent turf could take over. However, experts found that the nurse grass competed for space and nutrients, thus slowing the permanent grass, or even preventing its establishment. Annual ryegrass and redtop were much used for nurse grass, but the ryegrass was found to be overly aggressive, and redtop often carried a few unwanted species, such as timothy, with it. Sometimes as much as 25 percent or more of this nurse grass is still found in cheaper blends of grass seed. Today, fine fescue in a bluegrass blend serves as a nurse grass and has the added advantage of being useful as the lawn continues to develop.

What are the advantages and disadvantages of having white clover in the lawn?

White clover is an excellent companion of Kentucky bluegrass. The nodules on its roots trap nitrogen from the air and thus enhance soil fertility. However, clover is patchy in the lawn. It is especially disruptive when the white flower heads form and attract bees. Clover foliage is soft compared with grass,

Ann Reilly

White clover is patchy in the lawn, is likely to stain clothing, and dies back in winter.

Most seed companies offer mixtures for shade that are formulated for the needs of specific geographical areas.

so it may be slippery underfoot and likely to stain clothing more readily than would grass. Clover leaves die back in winter and do not, therefore, provide the continuous green cover of cool-season grass foliage.

What grasses are recommended for shade?

Essentially the same species are planted for shade as for sun, although the proportion of shade-tolerant types may be increased in the seed blend. Grasses perform better in the shade if helped by tall mowing and more frequent fertilization and watering. Rough bluegrass (*Poa trivialis*) adapts well to moist, shady spots. Although attractive, it is shallow-rooted and thus does not wear well. Do not sow it where there is much lawn traffic. Fine fescues are good for dry shade. All southern grasses except Bermuda stand shade reasonably well. Most seed companies now offer mixtures for shade that are formulated to meet the needs of specific geographical areas.

Are timothy and other farm grass species suitable for lawns?

Hay grasses are better left to the pasture and hay field. In the lawn they become coarse and clumpy. There's one exception to this: These sturdy grasses can be used in difficult sites where survival of the finer grasses is questionable.

Positive Images, Jerry Howard

Ground covers provide dependable, often evergreen, blankets of growth in areas where grass may not thrive, or where mowing is difficult or undesirable.

In Georgia, can I make a good lawn in a wooded area?

Spread a layer of manure, compost, or rotted oak leaves, together with some balanced lawn fertilizer, over the area. Spade or till this and rake level. Then in October or November, sow Italian ryegrass for a winter cover until warm weather. In the spring, plant sprigs (see page 11) of St. Augustine grass in rows about twelve inches apart. Water well, as growing grass needs a great deal of moisture.

What grasses are best for winter color?

Southern lawn grasses turn dormant and brown when the temperature nears freezing. For persistent green in winter, lawns must depend almost entirely on grasses introduced from Europe, such as the bluegrasses, fescues, bent grasses, and ryegrasses. In the South, sow ryegrass or a mixture of these cool-season species for a green lawn. In the North, the same grasses remain green much of the winter and turn brown only when exposed to drying winds or bitter cold. Lawns adequately, but not excessively, fertilized show better late color (see pages 30–34).

How much grass seed should I buy for 1,000 square feet of lawn?

Recommendations are usually printed on the containers. In general, these recommendations call for up to six pounds per 1,000 square feet for mixtures that are mostly ryegrass and red fescue, five pounds for 80-percent mixtures of these two, four pounds for 60- to 80-percent mixtures, and two to three pounds for bluegrass mixtures.

Why are there such differences in seeding rates?

There are several reasons for this, but the chief one is the size of the individual seeds. Bent grass seed runs about 8,000,000 to the pound; fescues, over 500,000; Kentucky bluegrass, 1,000,000 or more; and ryegrass, about 250,000. The more seeds to the pound, the fewer pounds needed.

Is there any grass that will stay green the year around in New Mexico?

In regions with sufficiently cool summers, yet not too extremely cold winters, Kentucky bluegrass stays green if well watered.

What grasslike ground covers other than grass can be used?

Much more on this later in the book (see pages 85–91). But for now, think of the creeping broad-leaved species, such as ivy, which make excellent ground covers. Of them, only dichondra needs seeding and mowing like lawn grass. It is pretty well confined to southern California. Creeping legumes, such as white clover, are acceptable for warm-weather cover, but are generally not favored because their blossoms and leaves add unwanted contrasting colors to the lawn.

What could we plant in April on bare ground that would be lawn enough for our fifteen-month-old son to play on by June? It needn't be a permanent lawn.

This question will make lawn lovers cringe, since the only answer is to recommend planting either of two species generally disfavored—timothy or oats. Both will cover the ground with a rough, haylike coating that can be mowed. The only other possibility is perennial ryegrass, which makes a very good temporary turf that will last a couple of years.

SPREADING THE SEEDS

Once you have chosen the type of grass seed you want, and have fed, graded, and lightly rolled the seedbed, it is time to spread the seed. Since you've put a lot of time and energy into getting the seedbed prepared, this is no time to save a few cents or a few minutes. Here are some guidelines:

- Buy high-quality seed. You may think it expensive, but you will also find that it has a large quantity of good seed in it and few weeds or cheaper seeds, such as annuals. Be sure the species of grass seed is suitable for your geographical area and your lawn conditions. Usually, garden centers carry the seeds most adapted to the area.
- Give the area a final raking, so it will be loose enough to accept seed.
- Don't skimp when spreading the seed. If the recommendation is for four pounds per 1,000 square feet, use that much. A thick growth will leave less space for weeds.
- After spreading the seed, scratch it in lightly with a steel garden rake, in an effort to cover it with no more than one-half inch of soil. Then, with a light roller, roll in two directions to assure good seed-to-soil contact.
- Sprinkle water over the area immediately after seeding, and never let the soil become dry until the grass is growing well. This may mean watering as many as three times a day. Do not water heavily enough to erode the soil or the seeds, of course, but supply enough water to keep the top inch of soil moist.
- Don't be surprised if a few weeds emerge. Weeds are annuals, and you can avoid future generations of them by mowing them before they go to seed.

I'm in a hurry to get my lawn planted. After I have prepared the soil for the lawn, is there any reason to wait before sowing?

It is best to wait a week between preparing the soil and spreading the seeds. After this period of settling, use a rake to

A shoulder-carried spinner spreader, useful for both seed and fertilizer applications.

remove low spots, debris, or clumps of vegetation you missed earlier.

Grass seed is expensive. How can I be certain that I'm spreading it evenly?

You should have two aims. One is to get the seed scattered evenly; the other is to get as many seeds as possible to germinate.

Before seeding, rake the topsoil surface again to make small furrows that will accept seeds.

If your lawn is small, you can scatter seed by hand. The seeds will be visible, so you can check for spots you missed.

For a larger lawn, use a mechanical spreader, which can be rented or purchased at a garden center. We recommend a shoulder-carried spinner spreader, which allows you to scatter the seed by turning a crank. You can use a push spinner spreader, the type often used for spreading commercial lawn fertilizers, but its wheels will leave tracks in the seedbed. To get a more even spread of the seed, mix it well with an equal quantity of some material of similar size, such as sand.

Divide the mixture into two equal amounts. Spread half the seed mixture by walking back and forth—east and west, for example—then spread the remainder walking the other way—north and south.

Scuff the seed in with a steel garden rake or a landscaping rake (see page 9). A few seeds will still be seen, but most of them should be covered in the top half-inch of soil. Roll the lawn twice, going in different directions, as in seeding. Then water, using the finest of sprays, so that the seeds are bedded down in the soil, but no soil is washed away.

A final thought on seeding: Select a windless day. It's impossible to spread grass seed consistently when even a light breeze is blowing.

Does a new grass seeding need protection?

Protection is essential only in special cases, such as steeply sloping ground or a poorly prepared seedbed that leaves the seed perched right at the surface. Most grass seed sifts into soil crevices where it is hidden, and it is too small to tempt birds. However, any seeding will benefit from a protective mulch, more to keep the seedbed moist than to protect the seed. A surface blanket of any inert material that is open enough to let sprouts emerge and permit moisture to soak into the bed makes a good mulch. Straw, a few straws deep, is widely used where it can be procured inexpensively, as well as such materials as excelsior, finely chopped twigs, grass clippings, sphagnum peat moss, and woven nettings. Mulches such as these break the force of rain and help both to prevent soil wash and to keep the seedbed moist. Seed will sprout quickly only if kept continuously damp. A mulched seeding requires less frequent watering

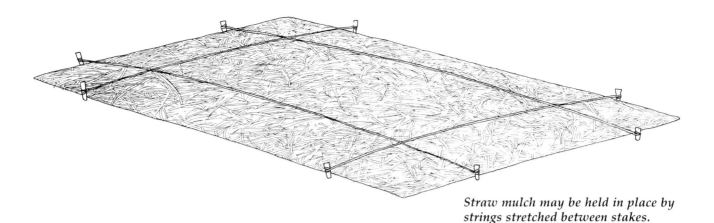

Straw mulch may be held in place by strings stretched between stakes.

than one exposed directly to air and sunshine, and thus usually makes a stand more quickly.

How do you lay the mulch down?

Mulches must be thick enough to retard evaporation of moisture but loose enough not to interfere with water penetration or seedling growth. Mulches that will not easily blow away in the wind and that decay naturally, so they do not have to be removed later, have advantages. On the whole, nothing has proved much more satisfactory than straw. Most of the time, a straw mulch stays in place if you walk on it to press it down. In especially windy spots, it can be held down with string tied between stakes. Excelsior is another excellent mulch. Hay is sometimes used, but has the serious shortcoming of containing a lot of weed seeds, which drop into the seedbed and quickly sprout and take root.

Is mulching a large area feasible?

Machines have been developed for mulching large areas, such as newly seeded roadsides. Some blow straw combined with an asphalt "tack" that binds the straw. Other hydraulic seeders pump on a mulch that is a slurry, made usually of woodpulp fibers. These machines can cover acres per hour. Many landscaping services have smaller versions, which can be engaged for custom service.

Is it all right to sow seed in the winter?

Seed will not sprout until warm spring weather. But this makes no difference. It is good to get the seed in place as soon as you can, since it may work down and become better imbedded in the soil from the freezing-thawing cycles. Old almanac advice was to sow grass seed on the "last snow of the year." One warning on this: Don't sow the seed where it might wash away; better in such areas to wait until warmer weather. And remember, use this method only if it is essential that you start your lawn in the spring. It's better to postpone the job until fall if you can.

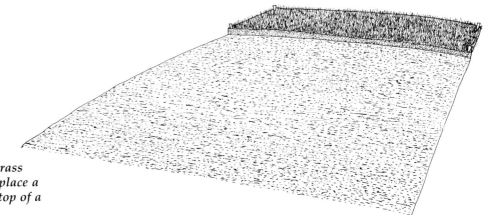

To help control erosion until grass seedlings become established, place a strip or two of sod across the top of a steep slope when seeding.

Are there any special precautions for seeding slopes with grass seed?

First, because of the obvious problem of erosion, consider sodding rather than seeding (see pages 22–25). Even a strip or two of sod across the top of the slope will help to control the soil from eroding. A seeded slope should receive protective measures, including ryegrass in the seed mixture, getting roots down quickly, and application of a good mulch. In the case of truly steep slopes, grass may not be the solution, since not only will it be difficult to get it to grow, but it will also be difficult to mow. Consider planting ground covers, such as creeping junipers, English ivy, or myrtle.

I've seeded my new lawn. What next?

You must keep it moist until the individual grass plants have pushed their roots down into the soil. This often means sprinkling three times daily, so that the soil looks moist at all times.

Both at the beginning and when the tiny plants emerge, keep pets and children off the lawn. They're the biggest lawn pests at this point.

How should a new seeding be watered?

New seedings are best watered with a fine spray, frequently applied. Forceful watering, especially on an unmulched seedbed, disperses soil, preventing water penetration. Spray lightly, frequently enough to keep the seedbed moist without surface runoff.

What about sprinkler systems for lawn seedings?

An underground system activated by a time clock set for brief waterings at frequent intervals is most convenient. Systems using plastic components that don't require plumbing skills for installation are now available. If you use conventional aboveground sprinklers, set them along the edge of the seeded area and aim them so that each will cover a section of the new lawn. Take care with heavy sprinklers: Many of them apply water more rapidly than a newly seeded area can absorb it, and thus may damage a seedbed.

How quickly does newly sowed lawn seed sprout?

This depends both upon the kind of grass and the weather. Ryegrass is fast, sprouting in just a few days. Fescues are slightly slower, and bluegrasses and bent grasses are even slower, often taking as long as two weeks. Seed must be kept moist and warm for fast sprouting, and germination is most rapid when daytime temperatures get into the seventies. Seed can lie dormant in the soil during freezing weather and will sprout only very slowly in temperatures below 50° F. Still, for spring sowings, it is best to seed the lawn as early as possible, letting the seed imbibe water and begin the sprouting process even though much action won't be seen until warmer temperatures later in the spring.

When should a lawn be mowed first?

Before being mowed, seedlings need a good root system so that the tiny plants won't be torn out of the ground; but don't let the grass grow so long that it flops over. It should be rooted deeply enough to begin mowing when the grass is almost twice the height at which it will be mowed when mature (see page 38). The soil should be allowed to dry out sufficiently to avoid footprints and mower tracks in the seedbed and to prevent damaging the tiny plants.

We seeded a new lawn early this spring and have a good stand of grass. Should it be mowed or left to grow this year?

It should be mowed, but not shorter than two inches.

The new grass on my lawn looks so frail and tender that I hate to mow it. What should I do?

If the grass is three inches tall, by all means go over it with the mower, setting the blade for a two-inch cut. Rather than hurting the grass, this will help to spread the growth laterally, thus creating a tight sod. If you are raising any of the low-growing bluegrasses, you can set the blade as low as one-half to one and one-half inches without doing any harm.

My new lawn is full of weeds. Should I till it up and start over?

Good heavens, no. If you imported topsoil, the weeds are probably from seeds in that. Keep the lawn mowed all summer so that none of those weeds get a chance to go to seed, and chances are good that most of them will be killed by the late fall frosts. Above all, don't use chemicals on the lawn to get rid of the weeds. Some chemicals that would be safe when the grass is more mature might kill seedlings.

THE INSTANT LAWN: SODDING

One day bare soil, and the next, a green lawn with a tight growth of grass and nary a weed. It seems like magic. But it's easy to create by sodding rather than seeding a new lawn, even for those not experienced in such work. There are many reasons for buying sod rather than planting seeds.

- Within two weeks you'll have what looks like a lawn of many seasons of growth.
- You'll be spared the seeding of the new lawn; and the need for watering and nursing sod is less than when you plant seeds.
- You'll have no mud tracked into the house, no fight to keep the children and pets off the new grass for many months, no worries about how—or if—the grass will grow.
- You will start with a dense lawn, free of weeds.

It isn't a perfect method, however. For one thing, it can be expensive. Figure the space you must sod, then get a price from a sod dealer (listed in your phone book) or a garden supply center that sells sod. The figure quoted should help you to make a decision. The next step is to prepare the soil. Although you buy sod much as you buy carpet for your home, it's not as simple as laying a rug.

If you've found a source of sod, know the price, and are satisfied with the quality of the sod, it's time to get to work. The area to be sodded must be prepared exactly as the seedbed for a new lawn is prepared. That means creating rich soil for the roots of the sod—it definitely isn't enough simply to rake a clay or sandy soil, then hope the sod will grow on it. You may have to bring in soil, then enrich it with lime and fertilizer. The area should be graded, one to one and one-half inches below the desired surface level, then rolled.

Have the sod delivered only after the area is prepared. Do not store cut sod for more than a day or two and never allow it to dry out.

Positive Images, Jerry Howard

Sodding produces a mature-looking lawn more quickly than seeding, but it is expensive and, like seeding, requires careful soil preparation.

Sod is usually delivered in rolls. Prepare the area before delivery and never allow the sod to dry out.

Sod is delivered in squares or, more often, in rolls. Lay the squares or strips parallel, with ends staggered and edges pressed close together, and no overlap. Use a knife to cut it at corners or edges, such as walks or driveways.

Check where the rolls or squares meet. If one is too low, fill under it to bring it up to level. If there is any space between strips, fill with topsoil.

Roll the lawn in two directions with a light roller, then spray the grass, enough so that the water soaks through the sod and into the soil. Keep it moist for at least two weeks, until the roots are reaching down into the soil. Also, keep people and pet traffic off the grass during those two weeks. After two weeks, treat it as an established lawn. It may be time for mowing.

Is there anything to be wary about in purchasing sod?

Buy sod from reputable sources that identify the grasses. Look for weeds or inferior grasses. Ask for assurance that there are no pests in the sod, such as crabgrass seed or harmful insects. Sod

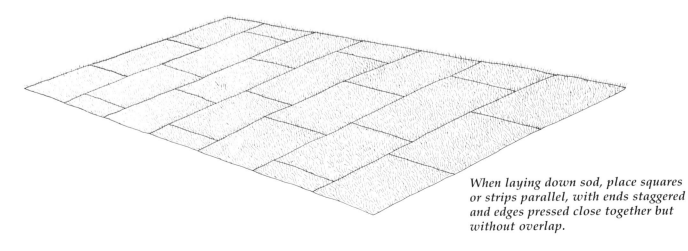

When laying down sod, place squares or strips parallel, with ends staggered and edges pressed close together but without overlap.

For best results, lay sod in early spring.

that is cut thin (one inch) roots most rapidly, but it also dries out more readily than thicker sod. Before accepting delivery, be certain that the sod is fresh and has not dried out. A yellowing sod is a sign of its drying out.

When should I lay sod for my lawn?

Early spring is the ideal time. New roots develop best during this period.

Does sodding make seedbed preparation less necessary?

Definitely not. Sod placed on poorly prepared soil will perform no better in the long haul than would a seeding given inadequate seedbed preparation. Before laying sod, add fertilizer and lime, if needed (see pages 30–36), loosen the root-zone soil, remove debris, and make sure that the site is level.

I have soil that is fairly heavy with clay. Since I plan to lay down rolls of sod, can I get away with merely leveling the surface?

No. Sod is little more than an inch thick. It must have a good layer of soil underneath it, so the roots will move down into the soil to obtain food and moisture. If it doesn't have these, the sod will, at best, not thrive, or it may eventually die.

I am going to sod a slope and will be buying rolls of sod. Should they go across or up and down the slope?

Lay them across the slope. Drive small wooden stakes into the ends of the rolls to hold them in place. Tamp or roll the sod lightly, since you want it to push roots down into the soil as quickly as possible. Then sprinkle the sodded area, enough to make certain the water gets down through the sod, but not enough to cause any erosion.

Must I take special pains with a newly sodded lawn?

Firm newly laid sod into the soil by light rolling with a lawn roller. Top-dress any depressions that are noted. It takes several weeks for the sod to reroot into the enriched soil beneath it. During this time it should be watered regularly and thoroughly enough so that not only the sod but also the soil beneath it is moistened. Care for it as you would an established lawn.

Are there less expensive alternatives to sodding?

Yes, small biscuits of sod, called *plugs*, or stem fragments, called *sprigs*, can be planted if available in your area (see page 11). Both will spread and form a tight turf within a season. Southern grasses for which no seed is available are often planted this way. Sprigs will give more coverage than an equivalent weight of plugs, but sprigs dry out quickly, so they require immediate planting. Zoysia sprigs spread a bit more quickly than do plugs.

Even so, zoysia is so slow-growing that a year or more is required to make a solid stand. On the other hand, Bermuda grass makes a stand in just a few weeks. Other southern grasses fall between these extremes.

Are sodded lawns or lawns planted from sprigs or plugs preferable to seeding?

You can get an argument on the answer to that question. The only advantage of sodding is quickness in providing mature turf. The advantage of sprigging or sodding is the perpetuation of cultivars that don't come true from seed. Sod may forestall weed appearance, but the potential for weeds is still in the soil if the sod fails. Such vegetative planting risks the introduction of pests and diseases more than does direct seeding. Some experts feel seeded grasses—rooting directly in home soil—do better than grass that is transplanted.

Can grass fragments be used to start a lawn?

Yes, this is possible with some grasses, particularly creeping bent grasses and Bermuda grasses. Sod is shredded, or stem clippings cut, to make what are called *stolons*. These are scattered over a prepared seedbed just as is grass seed. Because these stolons dry out quickly, top-dress them immediately with about a quarter-inch of soil, or press then firmly into the ground. The new stolons must be watered without fail until roots develop at the joints and new growth appears.

Must colonial bent grasses be started vegetatively (by sod, sprigs, or plugs)?

No, colonial bents such as Highland are available as pure-line seed. Colonial bents do not require the intensive care that the lower-growing creeping bent grasses do. Colonial bents are best mowed at a three-quarter to one-inch clipping height.

REBUILDING A LAWN

In the preceding sections, we emphasized the importance of doing a good job when creating a lawn. It is a lot of work, but the dividends are great: You will have a lawn of which you will be proud, and you will have far less work keeping it in excellent condition.

This section explains what you must do to rebuild an existing lawn. Those facing this job, as well as those who are getting ready to create a lawn, should understand one point: It is more work to rebuild a lawn than to do the job right the first time.

Why is this?

First, although the soil is poor, the lawn may be up to grade—that is, the lawn is at the level you want it in relation to your house, walk, and drive. Some of this earth must therefore be removed to make room for the addition of good topsoil. Second, the soil that is there is probably heavy with undesirable grasses, weeds, and weed seeds. You must get rid of these before you can rebuild your lawn.

The first step is to make a decision about the soil now in place. You must have a minimum of three to five inches of rich soil. If you have a layer of sand or clay on which you have been unable to grow grass, you may decide to bite the bullet and replace that top layer. If your lawn is average size or larger, this means arranging for mechanical equipment, such as a bulldozer or front-end loader, that can quickly scrape up and truck away the unwanted layer.

Then you must have topsoil brought in. To figure how much soil you need, estimate about one cubic yard of topsoil to spread a four-inch layer over eighty-one square feet. After this topsoil is spread, follow the instructions given earlier for a new lawn (see page 10).

In some cases, however, you may decide that even though your soil is poor, it can be improved and need not be replaced. Your first step is to test the soil with a soil-testing kit or by sending a soil sample to your Extension Service. The results of the test will indicate what types and amounts of fertilizer are needed. Phosphorus will almost certainly be recommended, since once it is in the soil, it stays at just about the same level. This is your opportunity to work it down to the level where the roots will benefit from it. You may find that your soil also needs nitrogen and potassium.

Don't wait for the test results to begin work on your lawn. First, rototill it, with the aim of destroying all vegetation, grass, and leaves that are there. Rake up all of this material—it's fine for your compost pile.

It's best to wait three weeks after tilling. During this time, bits of turf or hidden weeds will begin new growth. Rake them up. Before taking the next steps, you should be satisfied that none of the old growth will emerge.

You now have an opportunity to make soil improvements that will last for years. Add organic materials, such as chopped hay, leaves, rotted sawdust, rotted manure, compost, and peat moss, to the soil. These will help sandy soils to retain moisture and improve clay soils by enabling them to become more permeable to water and air. It is difficult to overdo this step. From one to three inches—or even more—can be added.

After spreading on organic material, add the commercial fertilizer suggested by the test results, and rototill to mix all of this into the top three to six inches of the lawn area.

At this point, follow the same procedures for preparing the seedbed as those given earlier for creating a new lawn.

A rotary power tiller.

How do you renovate an old lawn infested with "devil grass"?

You've heard that a weed is simply a plant growing in the wrong place. Here's an example of it. Devil grass is Bermuda grass, chosen for lawns in California and Florida, but the very devil to get out when it moves into gardens or lawns made up of some other grass. Even a tiny piece of root will start a new plant. Try tilling the lawn several times, raking up the root pieces carefully after each tilling, then reseeding. The care with which you remove the roots determines your success.

I plan to rebuild my lawn to get rid of a huge crop of weeds. When should I do it?

Begin preparing your soil so that you are ready to sow the seed at the same time recommended for starting new lawns. In general, seed in the spring in the South, in the fall in the area from Philadelphia and Washington, D.C., west to the Plains, and in the fall (or, less desirable, the spring), in more northern areas.

One of the reasons why I plan to rebuild my lawn is the vast number of mushrooms that pop up every summer. Can I use some pesticide to make certain I will have no more of them?

That's not necessary. You'll be rototilling your area before starting your new lawn. Mark the areas where these mushrooms grow. When you rototill, look for logs, tree stumps, or pieces of lumber scattered when your house was being built. Remove these as you till, and you will eliminate those mushrooms.

The reason that I need to rebuild my lawn is the existence of a large wet area. What should I do about it?

First, figure out why the area is wet. If it is because your soil is clay (see page 6), improve the soil by adding organic material, such as leaves and compost, to lighten the soil and permit the moisture to go down into the subsoil. If it is simply a low area in the lawn due to improper grading, you can easily build up that area when you rebuild your lawn. If it is a more serious problem, such as a high water table or chronic seepage, you will have to put in drain tiles to carry away the water.

I got rid of a lot of weeds in my vegetable garden by raising a crop of buckwheat, then tilling it in. This also improved the soil by adding organic material. Could I do the same thing on my lawn, which I'm planning to rebuild?

You could, and it would work exactly the same way (see page 44). For example, in Massachusetts, where you live, raise a cover crop in the summer and then till it under. If you till it about three weeks before you want to plant grass, it will have a chance to begin to decompose. The grass seed can then be sown on a vastly improved seedbed. There is one big question for you, however: Are you prepared to live with what would amount to an unmowed lawn for most of a summer? Perhaps equally important, are your neighbors prepared for this?

2 *Basic Lawn Care*

I f you have built or rebuilt a lawn according to the instructions given earlier in this book, lawn care need not be a chore to be avoided if at all possible. Certain procedures are required, however, which if faithfully carried out, eliminate the much more difficult work of bringing your lawn back to first-class condition.

Lawns must be mowed—as often as weekly when the grass is determined to grow. They must be fertilized. They must be watered in dry seasons, or allowed to go dormant and brown. Finally, they must be watched, to see that none of the typical lawn problems move in. If problems do occur, action must be taken quickly, before the problem reaches unmanageable proportions.

Keep a small notebook near the mower in the garage. Enter the hours spent mowing, so you will know when your mower needs a change of motor oil. Record your lawn feeding schedule, and note when you fertilize, along with the kind and amount of fertilizer you use. When you build or rebuild your lawn, jot down the name of the seed or mixture used, so that you can later judge its worth.

Tending a lawn is a form of instruction. In northern areas, for example, you will learn that leaves left on the lawn in the fall do not disappear; instead, they are there in the spring and the grass under them is in deplorable condition. You will learn that a mower in need of sharpening will tear at the grass and leave ragged edges that brown quickly. You will learn the value of doing a job well when you are paid off with an improved lawn.

◀ *At the height of the growing season a healthy lawn needs about 1 inch of water per week, which you must provide if the rains fail.*

What makes a lawn look good?

Good looks are due mainly to density, uniformity, and rich color of the grass plants. Planting improved cultivars helps greatly, but you must also mow regularly and eliminate weeds. Proper fertilizing will help achieve a deep color and keep the grass vigorous to help you fight weeds.

Let's take an example. You have a lush lawn with five dandelions growing in the middle of it. With a deep-bladed tool, you go out and get every trace of the tap roots of these invaders. Although you have eliminated the weeds, however, you still need to fertilize the lawn, since the best defense against future growth of weeds is a healthy growth of grasses.

Do maintenance programs differ for different kinds of lawns?

Yes, indeed. Some grasses require more attention than do others, especially the heavy feeders, such as Bermuda and bent. Fast-growing types, such as Bermuda, require more of just about everything, especially mowing and fertilization, than do a "poor man's grass," such as centipede, which actually suffers if fertilization is too generous. Some grasses, such as fine fescues and zoysia, can get by with little attention, but even they look better when well cared for. Zoysia is slow-growing and can stand infrequent mowing, but looks more attractive if clipped each week or so.

Must one treat a lawn differently in the South than one would in the North?

Yes. If Bermuda grass in the South is fertilized in July, it will be better able to compete with the weeds, whereas a seeding of grass in the North at that time might help crabgrass more than it does lawn plants.

What attention can an "average" lawn be expected to need in areas where bluegrass predominates?

Mow weekly, perhaps every five days at the height of spring growth and maybe each ten days during summer slowdown. Fertilize a few times annually, particularly in autumn for bluegrass. Possibly treat against broad-leaved weeds in the spring. Finally, water during dry periods.

FERTILIZING AND LIMING

Can you tell me what those numbers mean on bags of fertilizer?

Let's take an example and explain it. We see a bag of 15-5-10. This means that 15 percent of the contents of the bag is nitrogen, 5 percent is phosphorus, and 10 percent is potassium. The remainder is inert filler. Nitrogen stimulates the growth of plants; it produces vigorous growth and deep green color. Phosphorus helps in the development of roots and prevents stunting. Potassium helps to produce sugars and starches, the energy foods of plants, and helps the plants to resist disease.

The temptation when spreading these fertilizers is to use a little more than the recommended rate, figuring that if a certain amount is good, more must be better. Particularly with nitrogen, it simply doesn't work that way. Too much nitrogen at one time will contribute to disease, pollution, unnecessary mowing, and even burning. This often means that several applications of fertilizer will be needed in one season. An alternative is to purchase the more expensive fertilizers that are formulated to make the nitrogen available to plant roots over a longer period.

Why are there so many combinations of fertilizers?

To meet specific needs. The following table provided by the Extension Service gives only a few of the grades of fertilizer and suggests uses for them on the lawn:

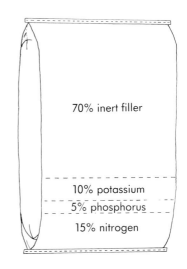

A bag of 15-5-10 fertilizer.

Choosing the Right Grade of Fertilizer

GRADE	WHEN TO USE
5-20-10	For lawns testing low in phosphorus
5-10-10	For lawns not regularly fertilized, or for preparation of a seedbed for a new lawn
10-10-10	For lawns in need of extra phosphorus and potassium, but not generally impoverished
15-10-10	For lawns fertilized regularly but in need of more phosphorus
15-8-12	For lawns fertilized regularly but high in phosphorus
20-10-5	May be used for a lawn pep-up; contains too little potassium for regular use and, because of the high percentage of nitrogen, may result in greater disease susceptibility

How much fertilizer should I use per year?

This is difficult to answer because of the many factors that must enter into the answer. For example, sandy soils require more fertilizer than clay soils, since some is lost through leaching. Also, more fertilizer is needed if you faithfully remove all grass clippings, rather than letting them gradually enrich the soil. You can cut the recommended amounts if you wish to save money, but too little means a thinner lawn—and the strong possibility that weeds will move in.

Use the accompanying table to start off, then change the amounts as you see how your lawn progresses.

A common recommendation for lawn fertilizer is a mixture with a nitrogen-phosphorus-potassium ratio of about 3-1-2. Thus, if you selected a fertilizer with 15-percent nitrogen, you would look for 15-5-10 on the bag.

Estimating the Correct Amount of Fertilizer

NITROGEN PERCENTAGE (first number on fertilizer bag)	TOTAL POUNDS PER 1,000 SQUARE FEET
30	15
20	20
15	30
10	40
8	50
5	80

When should I plan to feed my new lawn?

If you've done your preparation work well, adding both organic matter and fertilizers to the soil, you should not have to feed the lawn until the year after planting, when you should begin a program of periodic feeding.

When should I feed my established lawn with its recommended amount of fertilizer?

If you buy the bags of standard fertilizer, such as 10-10-10 or 20-10-5, you should probably divide the amount to be applied into four feedings. In most of the United States, the first feeding could be in early spring, the next two in the summer months (early June and late August in northern areas), and the last in early fall. Special lawn fertilizers have been developed that slow down the conversion of nitrogen into the nitrate form needed by the grass plants. Advertised as long-lasting or slow-release, these fertilizers are used in a single application, early in the growing season.

In the North, should I wait in the spring until my lawn is growing well before applying fertilizer?

No, it's better to spread the first feeding of fertilizer at least a week or two before the new growth begins. By doing this, the fertilizer will be available to the roots when the grass needs it most. It's best to spread the fertilizer on a dry day, then soak the lawn to wash the fertilizer off the top of the grass and down into the soil.

When should I fertilize my lawn in Florida?

Early in March apply a lawn fertilizer. Feed the lawn again when the rains start in June. In all parts of Florida except the extreme north, additional small monthly feedings in January and February help to keep the grass green through the colder months and build it up for its spurt of spring growth.

I need a fertilizer spreader. What type should I buy?

Use a grass seed spinner spreader, either shoulder-carried or push type (see page 18). Both throw fertilizer from a spinning disk. The common drop-spreader doesn't handle granulated fertilizers well, is hard to clean, rusts quickly, and is difficult to adjust for even and accurate spreading.

For fertilizing small lawns, the shoulder-carried spreader works fine. Not only is it easy to use and clean, but since it spits out fertilizer for fifteen feet, it will do a small lawn in minutes. Because the fertilizer is metered through a single large opening, it is easy to measure the amount being used. Also, there's little problem with the striping that sometimes appears on a lawn after improper use of a drop-spreader.

The push-type spreader is really a large can mounted on wheels, with the fertilizer being fed from the can onto the spinning disk. It can be used for lime as well as fertilizer.

I can't get my fertilizer spreader to measure the amount it disperses accurately. What should I do?

Mark out a square foot on your driveway. Measure one teaspoon of the fertilizer, and spread it evenly across this square foot. That is how ten pounds of fertilizer per 1,000 square feet will look. If you are spreading at twenty pounds per 1,000 square feet, measure the square foot and spread two teaspoons. Now fill your spreader and try to duplicate the density of the sample as you fertilize your lawn. When you've finished, estimate the amount of fertilizer you've used and figure how much you've used per 1,000 square feet. You can use these calculations to set your spreader for a more accurate spreading the next time you use it.

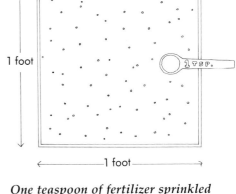

One teaspoon of fertilizer sprinkled over 1 square foot demonstrates the density of fertilizer necessary to apply 10 pounds of fertilizer to 1,000 square feet.

Last year I fed my lawn well, and the results were good all season, but my drop-spreader left lines of deep green where I fertilized—and much lighter areas where I missed. How can I avoid this?

I expect that you measured out exactly the amount of fertilizer needed for your lawn, loaded the drop-spreader, and then pushed it along, dropping a fairly heavy amount of fertilizer as you went. With drop-spreaders, it's best to set the amount being applied at a low figure, then apply half of it in one direction and half at right angles. If you haven't used it all up, go diagonally on a third trip.

Will lawn fertilizers help the trees?

They certainly will. A tree on a fertilized lawn will probably grow twice as fast as its unfertilized counterpart. Some gar-

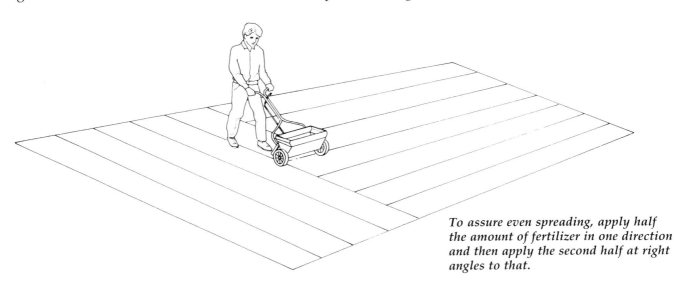

To assure even spreading, apply half the amount of fertilizer in one direction and then apply the second half at right angles to that.

deners prefer to place fertilizer more deeply in holes bored in the soil around the periphery of a tree to encourage its growth. Fertilizer compressed into spikes that can be driven into the ground with a hammer is available, eliminating the need to bore holes.

How shall I fertilize, water, and care for a lawn of centipede grass?

Centipede grass (*Eremochloa ophiuroides*) is one of the best lawn materials for the light, sandy soils of Florida. An application of a lawn fertilizer in March and another in June or July should suffice. Water the fertilizer in as soon as it is applied, and irrigate often enough to keep the grass leaves from curling and turning gray-green. Frequent mowing is necessary for a good centipede turf. During the growing season, the mower must be used at least once each week.

Why is pH so important?

pH is a scale used to measure how sweet (alkaline) or sour (acid) a soil is. It is measured on a scale of 0 to 14, with 7 being neutral. The reason that pH is so important is that even where nutrients are present in soil, plants can't absorb those nutrients if the pH is too high or too low. The pH test will not tell you, for example, if there is enough phosphorus in the soil, but it *will* indicate whether the soil conditions are too acid or too alkaline for that nutrient to be released.

Soil acidity not only directly decreases the availability of elements, but it also reduces the activity of soil bacteria: at 4.0, such activity may even cease completely. Also, some toxic elements, such as aluminum, are released at both a low pH (below 5.5) and a high one (above 8.5).

The pH scale measures how sweet (alkaline) or sour (acid) a soil is. On a scale of 0 to 14, 7 is neutral. Most lawns, flower beds, and vegetable gardens do best in a soil with a pH of 6.5 to 7.

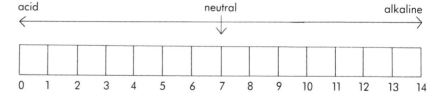

How can I know how much lime or sulfur to add to my soil to get the correct pH?

Your first step is to test the soil to determine the present pH. You can have this done by your Extension Service or do it yourself with an inexpensive kit. You must know, too, whether the soil is sandy loam or heavy clay loam (page 6). With those facts in hand, you're ready to apply lime or sulfur.

To raise the pH a full point, such as from 5.5 to 6.5, apply thirty-five pounds of ground limestone to 1,000 square feet of sandy loam, fifty pounds to medium loam, and seventy pounds to heavy clay loam.

To reduce the pH a full point, such as from 6.0 to 5.0, apply ten pounds of dusting sulfur per 1,000 square feet of light sandy loam; fifteen pounds on medium loam, and twenty pounds on heavy clay loam.

What is the ideal pH?

The homeowner with a lawn, flower beds, and a vegetable garden will do well to aim for a soil pH of 6.5 to 7. Most grass seeds will not tolerate soils with a pH below 5.5, and most garden crops need a pH above 6. Similarly, most flowers do best in soils of 6.5 to 7. A few shrubs, such as azaleas, do best in more acid soils (from 5.5 to 6.5). You can isolate such plants by growing them in raised beds and applying sulfur to lower the pH of just that one spot.

What is the action of lime on a lawn?

If the soil is heavy, lime will help to allow air and moisture to penetrate. Lawns tend to become acid in rainy climates, and most fertilizers are mildly acidifying. Lime will counteract this tendency. The importance of this is that if the soil becomes too acid (too low a pH), the plants are unable to use nutrients, even though they are available in the soil. For example, nitrogen is not available to plants below about 4.6 pH; phosphorus at 4.7, and potassium at 4.9. Thus, while lime is not a fertilizer, in acid soils it can have the effect of a fertilizer by unlocking nutrients in the soil and thus making them available to plants.

Are wood ashes good for the lawn?

Wood ashes supply lime (as well as potassium) to a lawn. It is fairly difficult to spread ashes evenly on a lawn, so many save them for the garden. Long-time burners of wood have discovered something about using wood ashes: It's very possible to overuse them if you spread them on the same soil year after year. The soil, even in the most acid of areas, simply becomes too sweet (has too high a pH), in which case you might have to reverse the action by adding sulfur to the lawn (see page 34).

I have fertilized my lawn regularly for many years, but for the past couple of years the lawn seems to have deteriorated, despite the fertilizer. What could be wrong?

Since you live in southern New York, you're in an area where the soil is acidic (has a low pH). Acid soil prevents the nutrients from being taken up and used by the grass plants. Unless lime is used on them, lawns tend to become increasingly acidic.

How do I know how much lime my lawn needs? I have never limed it, and there are signs of moss cropping up in it.

This answer applies only to areas of the country, such as the Northeast, where the soils are acid. Lawn soil becomes increasingly acid from leaching (a process in which water percolates through the soil, washing out soluble matter) and the removal of grass clippings. Sandy soils require light and frequent liming. Clay soils require heavier but less frequent liming. Pulverized, or ground, limestone, is inexpensive and easy to spread, although ground limestone is dusty and therefore messy to handle. Dolomitic limestone, if available, is good to use. Test your soil to determine whether it needs lime. Overliming can cause your grass to suffer from a tie-up of some micronutrients, such as boron, iron, manganese, and zinc, so they aren't available to the grass plants. Plan on liming the lawn every second or third year. If you haven't limed in three or more years and your soil tests acid, apply fifty to eighty pounds per 1,000 square feet.

Is it necessary to acidify alkaline lawns?

Sulfur, which acidifies, is less commonly needed than lime, which alkalizes, but it may be required in salt marshes, arid regions such as Western deserts, and areas with limestone bedrock. Depending on the degree of alkalinity, ten to fifty pounds of sulfur per 1,000 square feet may be needed. However, the problem is often one of sodium excess and not just alkalinity. Gypsum (calcium sulfate) is a better corrective for this than sulfur. Sulfur may be applied using the same techniques as one uses to spread lime.

My lawn needs both fertilizing and liming. Is there any reason why I shouldn't do them both on the same day?

There is. If you combine the two, you will cause a chemical reaction in which ammonia is lost and phosphorus becomes fixed, making it unavailable to plant life. Instead, apply the fertilizer, wait until rain or sprinkling has washed the fertilizer down into the soil, and then apply the lime.

WATERING

The water needs of a well-kept lawn do not vary greatly from species to species, although certain grasses, such as buffalo grass, are more able to endure prolonged droughts. At the height of the growing season any flourishing lawn needs about an inch of water per week. This must be provided by rainfall, irrigation, or stored moisture in the soil. Location in part determines this need. Sunny, windy spots in the deserts of the Southwest, for example, lose far more moisture than a protected lawn in the North.

Soil types, too, have an influence. The top foot of heavy soil, such as clay, can hold three inches of moisture, while a sandy soil will hold perhaps only half an inch. When watering, keep this difference in soil capacity in mind. Sprinkling a sandy soil with more than a half inch of water will be a waste, whereas clay should be watered slowly for a prolonged time until two or three inches of water have saturated the soil to the root zone. A cursory, nightly after-dinner sprinkling with the hose may relax the person sprinkling, but it does little to improve the lawn.

Why do lawn specialists criticize watering lawns every evening?

Because it does no good and, in fact, can cause harm. The roots of the grass should go down as deeply as possible in case of a drought. But if you give the lawn a light sprinkling every evening, the grass roots will stay close to the surface, where they are very vulnerable in a drought. As much as six inches of water is required to soak the soil to the depth where moisture is most needed. Check the penetration of water by cracking open the lawn surface with a shovel or a spading fork. If it is wet on only the top two inches, water enough to wet down six inches. Most of us are surprised how much water this takes—certainly much more than that twenty-minute after-dinner sprinkling.

Another potential danger with sprinkling the lawn in the evening is that the grass remains wet overnight and thus vulnerable to disease.

I'm always reading directions about how much to water my lawn. But how do I know how much water is being sprinkled onto it?

Place several coffee cans or a rain gauge in the area being sprinkled and measure the amount of water in them to get a good idea of how much is falling on the lawn. You need several cans to measure accurately, since most sprinklers tend to spread water quite unevenly. Generally speaking, you need to give about one inch of water in order to soak the lawn adequately.

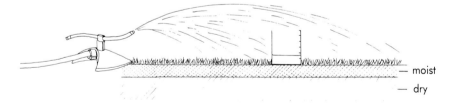

— moist

— dry

Use a coffee can to measure the amount of water you are sprinkling into your lawn. About 1 inch of water is usually necessary to soak the lawn thoroughly down into the grass roots.

I've been told the soil of my lawn is probably salty. How did it get that way and what can I do about it?

Soils become salty in arid regions where there is not enough rainfall to wash salts away from the roots of your grass. When salt is excessive, the roots are unable to take up moisture and nutrients from the soil. The salt can be from several sources, such as soil minerals breaking down, fertilizers, or irrigation water. It takes a lot of water to wash those salts down and out of the way—as much as twelve inches to move salts down a foot.

Is treated water all right for a lawn?

Any water suitable for general home use is harmless to grass, even if the water is heavily chlorinated. Muddy water from ponds is satisfactory for irrigation. In arid regions, where the soil is already quite salty, highly saline water from wells could worsen the soil structure, especially if not applied heavily enough to leach completely through the root zone.

Can a new growth of grass be overwatered?

Definitely. While the roots need moisture, waterlogged soil is unfavorable to the root growth. To avoid overwatering, watch the surface of the soil and rewater only when it begins to dry.

Would a covering of peat moss over the grass in summer help to hold moisture and do away with watering?

No. Most water loss occurs as the grass blades transpire (exude water vapor from the surface of the leaves). Soil coverings do not, therefore, help. Moreover, thatch that normally accumulates is the equivalent—free of charge—of applied peat moss. Save your peat moss for mixing into the soil.

MOWING

How close or high your grass is mowed has a strong influence on the health of the grass itself. Some grasses—bent and Bermuda grasses, for example—are better adapted to low mowing. But, in general, reasonably high mowing, not less than two inches, benefits the grass. Disease is less severe and weeds are fewer. This is most likely because more green leaf is left to make food for the plant and because the roots of tall-mowed turf tend to reach more deeply into the soil, thus tapping into a greater soil mass for more moisture and nutrients.

What kind of a mower should I buy?

Most equipment dealers today recommend small tractors. If you have a very large lawn, they are good, but buy a mower that matches your lawn size. If you have a small lawn, a hand-push unmotorized mower is perfectly adequate.

The reel-versus-rotary mower question has been pretty well settled in favor of the latter. Reel mowers have the advantage of cutting with a scissorslike action against a fixed bed knife and are highly recommended for low-mowed turfs that are well tended. These mowers are also somewhat safer than other types. Rotary mowers, on the other hand, are less expensive and easier to sharpen, adjust, and maintain than reels. They are also more versatile, able to get closer to walls and other obstructions, and because of the way grass is sucked up into the cutting chamber, especially useful for mowing tall, floppy grass.

No matter how sharp I keep the blades of my rotary mower, they seem to tear rather than clean-cut my grass (*Zoysia japonica*). The result is that the grass tips look ragged and usually turn brown soon after being mowed. A neighbor suggested that I use a reel mower. Do you agree?

Zoysia tissue is unusually fibrous. Heavy-duty mowers are recommended, and a well-adjusted reel mower would mow it more neatly than a rotary.

What is your opinion of electric mowers?

They're best for crowded neighborhoods on early Sunday mornings, since their noise will rouse only the lightest of sleepers. These mowers start easily, require little maintenance, are usually less expensive than similar size and weight gasoline-powered mowers, and are fine for small lawns with few trees or other growth around which the cord must be carried. They should not be used on wet turf.

I need specific instructions on how close to the ground to cut my lawn. The neighbor on one side tells me one thing, the neighbor on the other side tells me another.

Use the accompanying chart to determine your grass's mowing height. The length of the grass depends on the variety of grass that you have. If you have a grass mixture, as most of us do, use the recommendations for the taller grass.

To estimate when your lawn should be mowed, mow when the grass is 50 percent taller than the indicated higher mowing height. As an example, mow Bahai grass to three inches just before it gets four and one-half inches long; in other words, cut one-third off of its height to bring it to its optimal length.

What if I can't keep up with mowing, due to rain or some other cause?

If the grass gets excessively tall, cut it back a little at a time, letting several days pass between cuttings. If a lawn is scalped under such conditions, the plants will be weakened and roots will fail to grow for many weeks. This is especially damaging in the spring when stored food has been used to make fresh leaves; eliminating this growth then may even kill the plants.

I've been told to cut our grass "high." How high is that?

Leaving two or three inches is a high cut.

Does it make any difference which direction I mow?

Not too much. Purists mow parallel to the street, so that the mowing lines are not seen by passers-by. Specialists also recommend mowing in different directions in subsequent mowings,

Mowing Heights for Various Grasses

GRASS VARIETY	MOWING HEIGHT (in inches)
Bahai grass	2–3
Bent grass	⅜–¾
Bermuda grass	½–1½
Bluegrass	2–3
Centipede grass	1–2
Fine fescue	1–2½
Ryegrass	1–2½
St. Augustine	1½–3
Tall fescue	2
Zoysia	½–1½

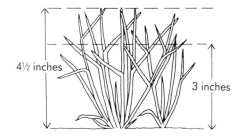

4½ inches   3 inches

Mow the grass when it is 50 percent taller than its optimal length.

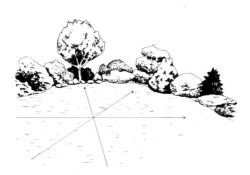

Change the direction of your mowing week by week to avoid "stripes."

saying that this will avoid a curved nap (a tendency of the grass to lean in one direction).

Should grass clippings be removed from the lawn?

This depends upon the kind of grass and how fussy you are about the looks of your lawn. Bent and Bermuda cultivars are very dense; these clippings should be removed because they won't sift down to the soil where decay is rapid. Clippings of most other grasses, if regularly mowed, are short enough to work into the soil unnoticed and even feed the lawn. If clippings are an inch or more in length and a heavy layer covers the lawn, remove them.

Are collected clippings of any value?

They certainly are. Because they are very high in nitrogen, they can be scattered in the garden or added to the compost pile. Whatever use you find for them, however, don't leave them in a heap on the lawn. If you do, they will heat up, become moldy very quickly, and much of their value will be lost. Scattered in a thin layer, they make an excellent mulch in the garden, adding nutrients and keeping down weed growth.

Thatch is building up on my lawn. What *is* thatch, and what should I do about it?

Thatch is a layer of dead material lying between the blades of grass and the soil. There are several schools of thought on what creates it: an accumulation of heavy layers of clippings left on the lawn, an overfertilization with nitrogen, or a drop in the pH that results in solid bacteria not being vigorous enough to break down grass clippings. Finally, those opposed to the use of

Ringer Corporation

Thatch is a layer of dead material lying between the blades of grass and the soil. Thatch-removal machinery can slice down through the sod, leaving the rooted grass plants in place, but removing quantities of thatch.

chemicals on a lawn believe chemicals kill off the microorganisms that would break down the thatch.

The chief problem with thatch is that it soaks up moisture. In even a fairly heavy rain, all moisture is held in this layer of dried grass as it would be in a sponge, never reaching the soil and roots where it is needed. In addition, disease organisms can grow in the thatch and cause major problems.

To get rid of thatch, first mow your lawn shorter than you usually do. If thatch is one-half inch or less in depth, try raking the lawn with a steel broom rake—the type used in raking leaves. If this doesn't remove the thatch, you can rent a machine that slices down through the sod and removes quantities of thatch. Since most of the rooted plants are left, the lawn will recuperate. This procedure is stressful on the grass plants, however, so do it before or during the period of most active growth. If it requires more than one treatment to remove the thatch, space treatments two or three weeks apart, and operate the equipment at right angles to the direction used the preceding time. An alternative to this method is to buy a lawn mower with a dethatching attachment. While this is not the best choice for removal of a heavy layer of thatch, such a mower, used regularly, will prevent any buildup.

I have just removed the thatch from my lawn. It was a big job and left the lawn looking quite messy, at least temporarily. How can I avoid having this thatch build up again?

In one respect, the presence of thatch is a healthy sign. It indicates a tight sod and hearty grass growth, both of which are good. One thing you can do to avoid excessive thatch is cut back a bit on the amount of nitrogen you spread on the lawn, so the growth will not be quite as lush. Second, and this is probably more important, remove grass clippings during the period of fastest growth. But, of course, don't throw them away. Work them into your compost pile or scatter them in your garden where they will enrich the soil.

Are there any "must" tasks for lawn care in the spring?

Spring is a time of year when both lawn-tenders and the grass have the urge to get up and get going. The first task should be to remove all winter debris—carefully. Don't use a stiff, steel garden rake; it will probably do more harm than good. Instead, use a broom-type steel or bamboo rake (see page 9), gathering leaves and other debris, but not trying to remove any dead grass. If you attack this job too vigorously, there's a good chance you will uproot many loose grass plants. If dead grass is really high, set your mower low and mow it before raking.

Another job to be done is to roll the lawn with a roller, smoothing out irregularities and making mowing that much easier all summer. Don't overdo the rolling. It can compact the

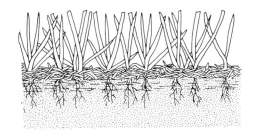

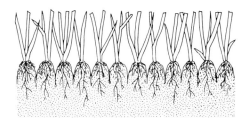

The turf above has thatch; that below is free of thatch.

OFF-SEASON CARE

soil and result in poor growth. In particular, avoid rolling heavy clay soils when they are wet.

If your lawn has any irregularities, this is a good time to fill in depressions by spreading a layer of sandy topsoil in the area. Don't use a layer more than one-half-inch thick. If more is needed, apply several thin layers, a week or two apart, so that you don't smother the grass underneath. Wait until the grass is up through one layer before adding another.

My lawn borders directly on the street. During the winter, the city salts the street during icy periods and plows after snowstorms. Result: snow and salt are tossed up on a broad belt of the lawn beside the street. Sometimes the grass revives, although slowly, but in one area it is dead. What should I do?

Usually, this doesn't require the addition of a fresh soil, since the salt should leach out during spring rains. In the spot where the grass hasn't revived, try working the soil down to a depth of at least one inch with a steel rake, removing the dead grass and exposing fresh soil. Seed this as you would a new lawn, roll or tamp it, and keep it watered until the new growth is firmly established.

Are there things that should be done to put the lawn to bed in the fall?

Only a few. Remove all leaves as soon as they come down and before snow falls. Raking is the usual method; push sweepers do the job more quickly. Rotary mowers with leaf mulching attachments are now common and efficient, chewing up the leaves

In the fall, all leaves should be removed from the lawn and the lawn should be mown until grass growth ceases.

Positive Images, Jerry Howard

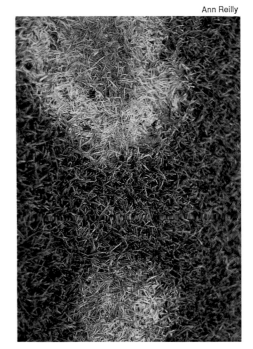

into tiny pieces that can be left on the lawn if there aren't too many. If there are a lot of leaves, however, remove them, and add them to the compost pile or spread them across the garden.

Continue to mow the grass until growth ceases. Your aim is to leave the grass short during the winter. This makes raking easier in the spring. It may also help to avoid snowmold, which appears as dead patches all over the lawn in spring. When the rest of the lawn begins to turn green, these spots remain black and dead. It is particularly common on bent grass or where the homeowner has failed to cut the grass close in the fall. Snowmold looks much like the spots caused when a pile of leaves kills the grass beneath it, but the causes are different. Although fungicides can be applied to the lawn in early winter, try going into the winter with a clean, short-clipped lawn, and thus avoid the use of these chemicals.

Last fall one of my neighbors dumped several loads of manure on his lawn and scattered it around. His theory is that the manure will feed nutrients down into the soil all winter. Is it a good idea?

I don't think so. All of the manure won't work down into the soil during the winter, which means he'll have a lot of manure removal to do come spring. In addition, the manure almost certainly contains weed seeds that will come up in the spring. Finally, it is almost impossible to spread manure evenly across a surface. This means that tiny sections of the lawn will be overfed with nitrogen, while other areas will receive little or none. Stick to commercial fertilizers from your garden store.

When winter comes, can I forget about my lawn?

Pretty much so, if you've given it a final good raking and mowing (and have carefully taken every last drop of gasoline out of the mower).

There are some things, however, that you should *not* do to your lawn during the winter. Avoid running paths across it even if it is covered with snow. If you have to shovel paths across the lawn, don't shovel all the way down to the grass; leave a blanket of snow for protection. Don't use salt to melt the ice off your walks or driveway; some of it will get out onto the grass, causing brown patches and thus extra work in the spring.

Grass left too long over winter may be invaded by a fungus disease called snowmold.

THE ORGANIC LAWN

Organic vegetable gardening has become increasingly common. Organic gardeners shun harsh chemicals or poisons to halt crop-destroying weeds, insects, or diseases because they know those chemicals may damage the very structure of the soil, with its thousands of microorganisms. Instead, they opt for naturally occurring materials, including compost (see page 107) and animal manures that will enhance the microbiological activity in their garden soil.

Blake Gardner

Organic lawn care entails conscientious maintenance; the best defense against weeds and disease is a healthy lawn.

Let's run through the steps of starting a new lawn organically, pointing out any differences from the conventional method.

Your greatest emphasis will be on preparing the area. If the lawn is to be at the site of a new home, avoid burying any trash in the soil and carefully remove any remaining on the surface.

Next, you must enrich the soil and at the same time improve its texture by adding organic materials in large amounts. These can be processed sewage sludge (a great source of nitrogen), bone meal (for phosphorus), and cottonseed meal, granite dust, or sheep manure (all good sources of potassium)—in short, any organic materials that are available in your area. If your soil is acid (see page 34), add enough lime to bring the pH up to a barely acid 6.5. Till all of this material into the top six inches of soil.

The next step—and one unique to organic gardening—is to raise a cover crop. Crimson clover and hairy vetch are common in the South; rye, winter rye, buckwheat, and field peas are just a few of the many that are popular in the North. All of these are called *green manures*. Start these in the spring, till them under when they're a foot or so high, and then wait four to six weeks for them to decompose before seeding your lawn. This process puts a large volume of rich organic matter back into the soil, often discourages weeds, and creates a fine seedbed that will be ready in the fall at exactly the right time for sowing a lawn in many areas.

Grading the topsoil, preparing it for sowing, and sowing the seed are the same for preparing organically managed lawns as for nonorganic lawns.

If you are committed to a nonchemical lawn, watch carefully for any signs of trouble—weeds, bare spots, yellowing or browning grass. Feed your lawn with organic topdressings, such as sifted compost. Mow it frequently, cutting only one-third or less of the grass blade length; in this way, clippings are short and can be left on the lawn to feed their rich nitrogen back to the grass roots. All of these good maintenance procedures keep grass healthy—the best defense against weeds and disease.

Is it better to grow a green manure crop in gray clay soil over the winter, or dig it under in the fall?

Fertilize the soil, grow a winter cover crop, and till it under in the spring. The area is then ready for grass seeding.

With commercial fertilizers, the contents' measurements are precise; you know, for example, exactly what you're getting in a bag of 5-10-5. Can organic fertilizing be that exact?

Usually not, and there's no reason why it should be. Organic gardeners—and lawnkeepers—aim instead to provide such an abundance of natural materials—including animal manures and green manures, composts and rock powders—that those major nutrients, N-P-K (nitrogen, phosphorus, and potassium) are always available, along with trace minerals and large amounts of organic material to lighten the soil.

Those not comfortable with this method, and particularly those accustomed to working with set amounts of commercial fertilizers, can work out similar fertilizer mixtures by using a chart indicating the percentage composition of common organic materials such as the following:

Nutrient Content of Common Organic Materials

	N	P	K
Alfalfa hay	2.45	.5	2.1
Wood ashes	0	1.5	7
Dried blood	12	3	0
Hair	12	0	0

I live near the ocean, so I can get seaweed by the truckload with very little effort. Should I use it, and if so, how?

Seaweed has been recognized as an excellent fertilizer for centuries, with generous amounts of nitrogen, phosphorus, and potassium. The exact amounts of these nutrients depend on the season and the variety of seaweed. It has the further benefit of being free of weed seed and plant diseases. Seaweed can be made the chief ingredient of your compost pile by mixing it with other materials, such as chopped leaves. Such a mixture, turned several times during the composting, will turn to a fine, black compost in as few as six weeks. Use it as a topdressing for your lawn by spreading it a half-inch thick, then working it under the grass blades with a steel rake. You can also spread it around shrubs or trees, or work it into the soil in a vegetable garden.

I have several large compost piles. I would like to use the compost as a topdressing on my lawn and add it to my garden soil as well, but will I be planting weeds in my lawn, since I compost all of the weeds out of my garden?

No. A compost pile built with some materials high in nitrogen will heat up to nearly 150°F. and will reach nearly this temperature even if you turn it to get the material on the outer layer into the center. This process kills weed seeds (see page 107).

Should topsoil be brought in if the soil is particularly bad?

Organic specialists usually say no to this for two reasons: You may be importing weed seeds, and you may be buying soil that is not much better than what you already have. Instead, enrich the soil that is there with organic materials, even adding bulky materials, such as leaves, that will greatly increase the percentage of organic material in the soil.

How do natural organic materials help the soil?

As the thousands of living microorganisms in the soil feed on the glucose that is released when organic material decomposes (breaks down), humus forms and enhances the soil for better plant growth.

Do I need to water my organic lawn as frequently as I would if it were nonorganic?

Because organic lawns tend to grow more slowly and to be hardier and more succulent, they may actually need less water.

Will I get thatch if I maintain my lawn organically?

Because organically managed lawns grow more slowly and there is increased microorganic activity in the soil, thatch is less likely to occur. Decomposition is able to keep pace with the dying parts of the grass plants that cause thatch build-up.

What kinds of natural controls can I use against insect pests?

Encourage birds into your yard by providing places for them to feed, bathe, and nest (see page 136). In addition, just as birds consume insect pests, so, too, do toads, snakes, and predatory insects such as lady bugs and spiders. Japanese beetles can be picked off your prize roses and dropped in a can of kerosene, and slugs can be lured away from your tender lettuce and peppers by placing saucers of beer in the garden.

INSECT PESTS AND DISEASES

It's amazing how many pests can eye your beautiful lawn with the worst of intentions. They range from the dogs and children in your neighborhood to the tiniest of growths—the molds.

First, however, a word of encouragement: No lawn anywhere has ever had all of these pests. In the next few years you probably will run up against two or three of them—not more. Furthermore, well-kept lawns do avoid most of the problems. For example, a thick growth of grass means there's no room for weeds. Crabgrass, particularly, loves to move in where it can find room, but will never be seen where the grass is thick. Keeping a lawn beautiful is much more satisfying than running down to the garden supply store each weekend for some chemical to solve the latest problem.

Pesticides are controlled by the provisions of the Federal Insecticide, Fungicide, and Rodenticide Act administered by the Environmental Protection Agency. Regulations change as to the legal use of specific pesticides. For this reason, we recommend that you check with a garden supply store to see what pesticide is available for a specific problem. Or, if you are in doubt about use of a specific chemical, call your local Extension Service agents. They are up on the latest EPA recommendations and can suggest what to try for specific problems.

The approach to these problems has changed in recent years. In the past, the recommendation was to find which chemical could be used to solve a particular problem. Today, the first approach is to see how the problem can be avoided, or if it appears, how it can be solved through nonchemical ways.

An example of this is the snowmold commonly found on many lawns in the North in the spring. This occurs when snow falls on unfrozen ground where drainage is poor and where grass remains under snow cover for a long time. It can be minimized by improving lawn drainage; by selecting grass seed that has proven to be hardy against threat of snowmold; by avoiding late, heavy nitrogen fertilization; and by cutting the grass in the late fall to prevent a mat of grass from developing. If none of these works, there are fungicides recommended by the U.S. Department of Agriculture that you can select.

When you do decide to use a pesticide, follow the precautions on the accompanying chart.

DO'S AND DON'TS WHEN USING PESTICIDES

- Carefully read and follow the directions for mixing and use.
- Pour liquid pesticides at a level well below your face in order to avoid splashing them onto your face or eyes.
- Be fully clothed when you apply pesticides. If the directions recommend them, wear goggles and a respirator.
- If you spill pesticide on your clothing or skin, remove your clothing immediately and wash your skin thoroughly.
- Don't use the same sprayers for insecticides and fungicides that you use for a herbicide.

- Don't use pesticides where there is danger of drift to other areas, such as vegetable gardens or patios.
- Avoid inhalation of the spray or dust.
- Don't apply pesticides on a lawn where people or animals are present.
- Don't permit children or pets on the lawn until the pesticide has been washed off by rain or sprinkling, and the lawn has dried completely.
- In case of contracted pupils, blurred vision, nausea, severe headache, or dizziness, stop using the pesticide and contact a physician.
- After using a pesticide, bathe and change your clothing. Don't eat, drink, or smoke until you have done this.

Lawn Pests and What Insecticides to Use Against Them
(as recommended by the U.S. Department of Agriculture)

LAWN PESTS[1]	DIAZINON	CARBARYL	CHLOR-PYRIFOS	TRICHLOROFON
Ants[2]	X	X	X	X
Armyworms	X	X	X	X
Billbugs	X	X		
Chiggers	X		X	
Chinch bugs	X	X	X	
Cicada killer wasps	X			
Cutworms[3]	X	X	X	X
Earwigs	X	X	X	
Fleas	X	X	X	
Fruit flies	X			
Grasshoppers			X	
Grubs[4]	X	X	X	X
Leafhoppers	X	X		
Millipedes	X	X		
Mites, clover	X		X	
Sod webworms	X	X	X	X
Ticks	X		X	

[1] Several insects are not listed because no control measures are necessary or chemicals for their control are not registered at this time. The active ingredients shown here are present in varying concentrations in many different commercial products.
[2] If only a few ant nests are present, treat them individually. Wash the insecticide into the nests or drench the mounds with it. For control of fire and harvester ants, consult your city or county Extension Service agent.
[3] To control cutworms, apply the insecticide in late afternoon.
[4] In hot, dry areas, use lower dosages to avoid burning the grass. Consult your city or county Extension Service agent.

My neighbor has a dog that is allowed to run loose over nearby yards, relieving itself at will. What can I do to get my lawn back in shape?

Dogs can be one of the greatest pests on lawns. Their feces are foul, unsightly, and disease-carrying. The urine of dogs is such a concentrated source of urea, ammonia, and potassium that it produces a toxicity similar to fertilizer burn. Female dogs are the worst offenders here, because they deposit urine on the lawn, producing a spot that will remain dead for most of a growing season. Cut out the dead spot with a shovel to a depth of six inches and replace with live sod from some less conspicuous area of your lawn. Press the sod firmly into place by stepping on it, then water well.

Moles are making a mess of my lawn. What can I do?

Moles, as you may have found out, like to dine on the bulbs in your garden. They also feed on grubs in your lawn. Use a pesticide to get rid of the grubs, and often the moles will move on to more productive hunting grounds. A second approach (if the laws of your community allow it) is to set mole traps, available in areas where moles are common. Moles live in burrows six to eight inches underground. When they burrow, they raise ridges on the surface of the lawn. To determine where to set the traps, roll or tamp these ridges. The following day, any new ridges are active ones—and good locations for traps.

My neighbor says mice are causing the winter damage to my lawn. In spots, it is bare down to the soil, and there is quite a bit of loose, dead grass scattered around. Is she right?

Probably. Mice live on the stems and leaves of grass as well as weed seeds in the winter, and may even girdle shrubs and small trees. Usually lawn grass will come back, so the only task is to rake up that dead grass in the spring. An ambitious cat is very helpful in this situation. Traps are useful but less effective.

Webworms are ruining my lawn. What can I do?

Webworms live in burrows deep in the sod, usually in the hottest, driest regions, and are seldom seen because they feed at night. They chew off the grass near soil level, leaving bits of grass and chaff, and saucer-shaped patches of brown in the lawn. Webworms are the larvae of lawn moths, which are frequently seen flitting over the lawn about dusk. At that time they are dropping eggs into the lawn. The cycle from egg to moth is about one month in warm weather, so that drenching the lawn with an insecticide about ten days after lawn moths are abundant should catch the larvae (the webworms). Webworms are seldom prevalent enough in the first generation to be a bother, but become damaging as populations build up during the summer. For this reason, plan on treating the lawn every two months, beginning in the late spring.

THOSE PESTY TERMS

Pesticide is a general term referring to a wide variety of agents used to kill or control plants, animals, or insects. Some of the more specific terms include:

Acaricide	mites and ticks
Avicide	birds
Fungicide	fungi
Herbicide	plants (more popularly known as weedkillers)
Insecticide	insects
Molluscicide	mollusks, especially snails
Nematodicide	nematodes
Ovicide	eggs, particularly insects in the egg stage
Rodenticide	rodents

How do I check chinch bugs?

These little fellows can do damage in impressive amounts. When they feast on grass, it turns off-color and eventually browns in irregular patches. Chinch bugs suck the sap from grass stems, debilitating and eventually killing the above-ground parts. The active insects will be found in adjacent green grass. Shake a handful of grass over white paper and look for white and black insects, some with red spots, not much bigger than a pinhead. Spray the undamaged turf well with insecticide.

Earthworms tend to leave castings on the lawn: should I try to get rid of them?

You can get rid of them through the use of insecticides that make the soil unattractive to these worms. They do leave castings, most noticeable on low-clipped turf such as bent grass. But before you declare all-out war on these fellows, consider their value. As they constantly work up and down, they improve the flow of moisture and air in the soil, enrich the soil with their castings, and consume thatch. On most lawns, they earn their keep, and their occasional castings should be forgiven or looked upon as topdressing. A quick brush with a broom rake will scatter these castings and enrich the surrounding soil.

The Japanese beetles are driving me crazy. They eat my raspberry bushes in the summer. Furthermore, their grubs attract skunks that dig up the lawn to feed on them. I want to eliminate them. How?

Eliminating Japanese beetles is almost impossible. It helps to understand the life cycle of this pest. The beetles deposit eggs in the sod during the summer. The young that hatch are small white grubs that grow strong as they feast on the roots of your grass. Those grubs go below the frost line during the winter, but return to the roots in the spring, then transform into pupae and adult beetles, which emerge to complete the cycle.

For the best long-term treatment, use a bacterial disease called milky spore, which can be purchased as a dust. Because introducing this disease into the soil of your lawn helps eliminate only the grubs, their wormlike larvae, and not the beetles that fly in, it is most effective when spread in large areas by community authorities. This disease is harmless to humans and other warm-blooded animals and to plants. It becomes more effective after several years, when it has spread through the soil.

One-time grub-proofing of lawns can be done with a diazinon-based pesticide available at your garden supply store. Don't use this together with milky spore disease, since the disease spreads faster if there is an abundance of grubs.

Traps are also available, which attract but do not eliminate the beetles. Picking the beetles, too, will help only to reduce the population. Spraying with carbaryl is also recommended.

It's a rare lawn that doesn't have a few weeds in it. The best defense against them is a lawn grown on rich soil, fed on a regular basis, and watered adequately, but not overwatered, so that the grass makes a heavy turf. It isn't necessary to run to the store for poisons to get rid of a few weeds. For example, dandelions can be dug up, if you're careful to go deep enough to get all of that lengthy taproot.

If weeds are beginning to move into your lawn, look for the reason. If your response is "yes" to any of the following questions, you have found your answer.

- To save mowing so frequently, have you "scalped" your lawn by mowing far too close to the soil?
- Have you failed to feed the lawn, so that the grass is getting patchy, leaving space for weeds to grow?
- Have you let your lawn grow too high, so that some weeds could go to seed?
- Did you plant your lawn with inexpensive grass seed containing a lot of weed seed?
- Do you have areas of the lawn that are always damp?
- Have you overwatered the lawn so much that the grass looks unhealthy?

I use weedkiller on my lawn and the beds around it, but every time I spray, I also kill or damage desirable plants. What am I doing wrong?

Follow these four rules to avoid that unwanted damage:

- Spray only on windless days.
- Get as close as possible to the unwanted weeds with the sprayer.
- Place a shield—either cardboard or plywood—in front of the plants you wish to protect, before you begin spraying.
- Use low pressure on your sprayer in order to keep the spray in a small area.

I have found an herbicide to use on the broad-leaved weeds that have found their way into my lawn. I hate to use this over all the lawn just to remove the weeds. Any suggestions?

It would be good if all homeowners had your reluctance to use pesticides on a broad scale. Reducing the amount of weedkiller used would also cut damage to other plants due to spray drift. For limited herbicide applications, attach a small cellulose sponge or a small (one-inch) paintbrush to a dowel or broom handle with a nail, tape, or rubber band. Pour the liquid weedkiller into a can, dip the brush or sponge into it, squeeze out the excess against the side of the can, then paint or sponge the weed. A single touch will do the trick.

LAWN WEEDS

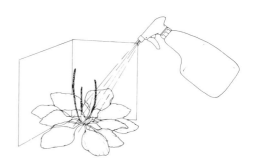

Place a protective cardboard shield behind plants you are spraying with an herbicide, get as close to the unwanted plant as possible, use a low pressure on the sprayer, and spray only on windless days.

To assure application of weedkillers on only the plant you wish to get rid of, dab the solution on with a small brush tied to a dowel.

COMMON LAWN WEEDS

Annual broad-leaved weeds include pigweed, mustard, ragweed, and lamb's-quarter. Although they make their debut in new lawns, they are usually not seen the next season, because in order to propagate, they must reseed. By mowing regularly, you interrupt this cycle. Don't bother to use chemicals on these; you may damage that crop of new grass.

Large, easy-to-kill broad-leaved perennials include some old "favorites," among them dandelion, chicory, dock, peppergrass, broad-leaved plantain, thistles, paintbrush, and sorrel. These plants form a low-growing rosette the first year, and thus duck under the threatening blade of your mower. Chemical control is necessary although digging may work if the population is small.

Ann Reilly

Broad-leaved plantain.

Small, creeping broad-leaved weeds offer a challenge—they're hard to defeat. You know them by the names of smooth chickweed, mouse-ear chickweed, knotweed, ground ivy, and clovers. They're perennial and will force their way into the best of lawns. Removing them by digging or pulling is almost impossible. Lime and fertilizer simply encourage them, and they can be cut shorter than grass without harm. Spot application of herbicides is the best treatment, but take care: The chemicals recommended for their control may injure lawn grasses as well as shrubs and trees with roots in the treated area. Repeat applications are necessary every year.

Annual grasses—goosegrass, foxtails, annual bluegrass, and worst of all, crabgrass—reproduce by casting seeds each summer and fall. The seeds overwinter in the soil and germinate in the spring. Discourage their growth by maintaining a vigorous, tight turf and keeping the lawn cut as tall as possible, so that the weeds are shaded out by the taller grass even if they manage to germinate.

Positive Images, Jerry Howard

Crabgrass.

Individual crabgrass plants may be removed by digging or pulling, but this is backbreaking when you are coping with crabgrass over a large area. Seedlings can be killed chemically, but a better approach is to use a preemergence herbicide (see page 53) early in the spring—before lilacs bloom. These chemicals work *only* on germinating seeds and will not kill crabgrass seedlings.

Perennial grasses include timothy, redtop, tall fescue, and other hay-type grasses. Maintaining a thickly growing sod will drive these out, but it won't trouble the most persistent of this family—quack grass. Some experts concede there is no control for this weed. Others suggest such drastic moves as covering the infected area with black plastic for a year. Quack grass, however, is known for longevity: Its seeds will lie in the soil four or more years and still germinate—and any pieces of rhizome quickly grow to hardy plants, with even more plants produced at each joint. In this way, the plant can quickly blanket and threaten all living things in a given area. Only persistent spading up of the plants, plus tilling in the fall, will help to keep quack grass under control.

Ann Reilly

Goosegrass.

I need some overall approach to weed control, to add some degree of sanity to my helter-skelter attempts to stamp them out. Any ideas?

Yes. It may help to consider all lawn weeds as falling into the five categories on page 52.

I've heard about preemergence herbicides. What are they?

There are two types of herbicides. *Preemergence herbicides* kill the tiny plants as the seeds germinate, but have no effect on living weeds. *Postemergence herbicides* kill only living weeds.

What are the most frequent lawn weed pests?

They vary from region to region. They are more diverse in the South, but individual species are more abundant in the North. Several broad-leaved weeds, particularly dandelion, plantain, chickweed, knotweed, and clover, are widespread in lawns, but can be chemically controlled. Annual grasses, such as crabgrass and foxtail, are abundant, too, and are best controlled with both preemergence and postemergence sprays. The perennial grasses, such as tall fescues and other forage species, are perhaps not as prevalent, but are really the worst lawn weeds because they are so difficult to control selectively. Ordinarily, to stop perennial grasses, a general herbicide that kills back all vegetation must be used, followed by replanting.

Can you dig weeds instead of using an herbicide?

Certainly—and congratulations for your ambition. When no selective herbicidal control is available, hand-digging works just fine, if there are only a few weeds.

I'm going to try to raise a lawn where there is nothing but quack grass. Any ideas?

Quack grass is a cool-season perennial that spreads by long, white underground stems as well as by seeds. If you try to till your area, you will only chop up those roots, and every one of them will form a new weed.

Author-gardener Dick Raymond suggests a way to get rid of this weed, but it takes a full season. His method recognizes that each of those pieces of root has only so much growing energy stored in it, and if this energy can be used up, the root will die and the quack grass will be eliminated. First, till the soil and then plant a heavy crop of buckwheat—three to four pounds per 1,000 square feet. As this quickly grows up, its leaves blanket the soil, discouraging the quack grass. When the buckwheat blossoms, till it in, and then plant another crop of buckwheat. When that blossoms, till it in; then plant a crop of annual ryegrass. This, too, blankets the soil, again preventing the quack grass from growing. The ryegrass will be killed by the frost and will blanket the soil during the winter. In the spring, till it in, prepare the soil for planting grass seed, and look forward to a lawn without a bit of quack grass and with soil enriched by those three crops you have tilled into it.

What can I do to prevent the spread of crabgrass?

A number of very effective crabgrass preventives are on the market. They are applied in spring before crabgrass seeds germinate, and affect only sprouting seeds. The materials, usually siduron or DCPA (dimethyl ester of tetrachloro terephthalic acid), must be used exactly as directed and spread uniformly to blanket the soil. Overapplication sometimes retards rooting of the permanent grass, so be judicious about repeated applications. Visit your local garden supply store for chemicals recommended for your area. You may also find controls for crabgrass that has sprouted, usually in spray form intended for two or three applications a week or ten days apart.

The surest way to avoid crabgrass is to leave no room in your sod for it to move in. In a one-on-one situation, a healthy grass plant can win over crabgrass.

I live in Oklahoma. Will you tell me how to get rid of Bermuda grass?

Grasses are extremely difficult to eradicate. An airtight covering of heavy building paper or old linoleum is effective. Also try persistent hoeing of the grass blades as they appear. Consult your county Extension Service agent concerning the use of herbicides.

A LIST OF DO'S AND DON'TS TO AVOID WEEDS IN THE LAWN

- Avoid weedy topsoil when starting or rebuilding a lawn. Some weed seeds are almost inevitable, but a check of where the soil comes from may help you to lessen this problem.
- Use good-quality grass seed. Inexpensive seed is likely to contain weed seeds and annual grass seeds. The annual grass will grow for one year, but won't come up the second year, and thus will leave lots of space for weeds.
- Sow grass thickly, according to instructions on the container.
- In the North, begin lawns in the fall for best results.
- Don't "scalp" a lawn by cutting it far too short. What is "short" depends on the grass you're growing (see page 38). Bent grass can be kept at putting-green height with no harm, and some of

the new varieties of bluegrass and ryegrass will tolerate closer cutting than the older varieties. In general, frequent cutting is better than close cutting. The worst thing you can do is to let the grass get four to six inches in height and then cut it as short as possible. A rule of thumb is to cut one-third the length of the grass. For example, let it grow to three inches, then cut off one inch.
- After the lawn is established, water only when the ground is dry, then soak it thoroughly. Frequent, light watering is a relaxing evening pastime, but it encourages shallow grass roots and the growth of crabgrass.
- Keep grass cut so that weeds don't have a chance to go to seed.
- Enrich the topsoil when creating the lawn, and feed the lawn on a regular basis (see pages 30–34).

Are there any natural controls for weeds?

There certainly are. Much weed management is based on an understanding of weed growth. For instance, many weeds grow in infertile soil, too acid or too alkaline soil, or poorly drained or hardpan soil. Rid your lawn of these weeds by improving the soil. Let us stress again that the surest way to avoid weeds is to create a good lawn from the beginning. Close-growing grass will crowd out most weeds. Organic gardeners thus have a rule for weed control in lawns: If weeds threaten, add fertilizer. They also warn against mowing too closely and excessive watering.

The summer night is hot. The lawn needs mowing—badly. Humidity is high, and for some unknown reason, someone has watered the lawn. Conditions are perfect—for a severe case of summer grass disease. The best treatment for these diseases is to avoid them by not overwatering or overfeeding the lawn in midsummer and by sowing more disease-resistant seeds.

Such diseases as brown patch and powdery mildew are much more common today with "improved" varieties of lawn grasses than they were in the days of unimproved bluegrasses. Bent grass is very susceptible and looks dead after an attack. It usually revives, since the roots have not been touched, but such an attack does open your lawn to an invasion by crabgrass and other fast-growing weeds.

Powdery mildew occurs in the fall as white powdery fungus on the outside of the leaf blade. This fungus sucks the nutrients out of the plants. Sunlight will stop it. Plant resistant cultivars, such as fescues and many cultivars of Kentucky bluegrass.

Red thread strikes lawns lacking fertilizer, appearing as tan to reddish irregular dead patches. Treat by feeding the lawn.

Melting-out, or *helminthosporium leafspot*, is caused by a fungus, and starts as reddish-brown or purplish-black spots on the leaves. Large areas of lawn are thinned out or killed as the grass crowns and roots die. It is most common on closely cropped lawns. Excessive nitrogen fertilizer, especially in early spring, will also increase the damage. The best attack is to plant a resistant variety of grass.

Pink snowmold and *gray snowmold* appear as irregular patches in the lawn in the spring. Snowmolds are caused by late fall fertilizing, a heavy mat of grass left on the lawn over the winter, snow falling on an unfrozen lawn, poor drainage, and long periods of snow cover.

Brown patch is a fungus disease that leaves brown, water-soaked areas during periods of high humidity. High nitrogen levels increase the severity of the disease, as does overwatering. Remove clippings from infected areas.

Pythium blight is another fungus disease caused by high moisture conditions. The infected area may feel greasy or have a

GRASS DISEASES

Ann Reilly

Ann Reilly

Some common lawn diseases: (top) powdery mildew; (bottom) fusarium blight.

fish odor; the grass is matted and lies flat. Do not overwater or feed too much nitrogen; remove thatch.

Fusarium blight is severe during hot, dry periods after early wetness. There may be light brown dead spots on the grass, or, if the crown of the plant is infected, the grass will turn straw color. Dead areas may have a spot of healthy grass in the center. Don't mow too closely, and, most important, don't let thatch accumulate.

Dollar spot appears as light tan dead spots on individual grass blades, followed by bleached out blades as the infected areas enlarge. Remove grass clippings and thatch, as the fungus that causes this disease can live on them for long periods.

There are pesticides to control these diseases. Unfortunately, most of them are preventive and thus must be applied before the disease appears and several times throughout the season. They call for extremely exact spraying. Because of the complexity of this treatment, seek advice from specialists such as Extension Services or lawn and garden centers.

What is a fairy ring?

The fairy ring is a circle of fungi—toadstools and mushrooms—that appears in the late summer or fall. The grass in this circle is greener than the surrounding turf because the fungi fix nitrogen from the air and the lawn grasses benefit from this. These rings develop from pieces of wood, perhaps a stump or a piece of discarded building lumber buried underground. The easiest way to get rid of a fairy ring is to find the wood—it will be in the center of the ring—and remove it.

Does disease enter through the sheared tips of grass blades?

Some diseases are thought to. In most instances, however, if conditions are right for a disease, it will find ways of infecting grass, mowed or not. But unmowed (and tall-mowed) grass has some advantage in resisting disease, probably mostly due to the extra food-making power of additional green leaves.

Will tree leaves injure a lawn?

Anything that obstructs light from the lawn will reduce the grass plants' food-making abilities. Tree roots, too, may reduce growth by competing strongly for fertilizer and moisture. But no toxicants occur in tree leaves that will appreciably inhibit the growth of familiar lawn grasses. Thus, the problem is mainly a mechanical one, not a chemical one. Small leaves, or larger ones shredded by a mower, should cause no difficulty in the typical lawn of bluegrass-fescue or other open-textured turf, if not more than an inch or two thick. The leaf fragments will settle into the grass foliage, which will soon overgrow them. When fallen leaves are so abundant as to smother the grass, they should be gathered for the compost pile or for mulching around shrubs.

Ann Reilly

Fairy ring—a circle of dark green grass caused by an infusion of nutrients in the soil where fungus is breaking down organic matter—can be disguised by fertilizing other grass in the area so as to deepen its color to match the ring.

Common Lawn Problems and Their Solutions

PROBLEM	SYMPTOM	SOLUTION
Ant hills	Small mounds of sand or dirt on the lawn that can spread over and kill the grass.	Use diazinon, following directions.
Broad-leaved weeds	See descriptions on page 52.	Apply general herbicides, as well as herbicides for specific weeds, such as dandelions. Follow directions exactly to get rid of these weeds.
Crabgrass	See page 52.	To prevent the appearance of crabgrass, use DCPA or siduron two weeks before the last expected frost. These are preemergence weed killers; postemergent herbicides are also available.
Drought damage	Many grasses, such as fescues, Bahia, Bermuda, and zoysia, turn brown, but live through all but the worst of droughts.	To protect plants during droughts, don't cut the grass closely and don't spread inorganic fertilizers such as 5-10-10. When you water, do so until water has reached to the deepest roots.
Fairy ring	As fungus in the soil breaks down organic matter, it releases nutrients and turns a circle of grass dark green.	Fairy ring doesn't harm a lawn, but you may wish to disguise its appearance by fertilizing well so that all the grass is the same color.
Fusarium blight	Patches of grass turn light green, then straw color, often with a patch of green in the center.	Rake out dead grass and reseed with resistant varieties, such as bluegrass. To prevent fusarium blight, treat the lawn with a fungicide containing benomyl or iprodione in late May.
Fusarium patch	Pale yellow areas, with pink along the edge, appearing in late winter and early spring.	At first sight of this fungus disease, treat with a fungicide containing benomyl or iprodione. Repeat after ten to fourteen days. Treat again in fall, during the rainy season when temperatures are below 60°F. Make two applications, two days apart. Keep the lawn mowed, to avoid matting.
Snowmold	See page 43.	Apply fungicides containing sulfur compounds such as maneb, ferbam, or zineb. These are most effective as preventives, but if infection is rampant, use them to help keep it from spreading further.
Grubs	In late summer, grass turns brown in irregular patches, and sod lifts up easily.	Grubs are the larvae of many beetles, such as Japanese beetles, which feed on grass roots. Use diazinon when you notice damage, then water well. Retreatment is often necessary. It may take up to a month to kill grubs.
Mole tunnels	Uneven, heaved up ridges in the lawn.	Moles feed on grubs. If you get rid of the grubs, you will no longer have moles. You can also try traps in active tunnels (those that reappear a day or so after being tamped down). Avoid using poison; it's too dangerous to have around children and pets.
Scalped spots	Caused by cutting grass too closely, shaving the tops of bumps in your lawn, or cutting the grass too closely after not mowing for an extended period.	Level high spots, set the mower higher, and mow more frequently.
Shade damage	Blades of grass are thin and dark green. Moss may be seen.	Prune overhanging trees and shrubs. Select shade-tolerant grass, such as fescues and some bluegrass varieties (Glade or Nugget) in the North, and St. Augustine grass in the South. Seed in fall and rake grass frequently to keep it free of leaves. If necessary, plant a ground cover such as English ivy, pachysandra, or periwinkle instead of grass.
White or gray cast to lawn	Caused by dull lawn mower blades, which chew into grass, tearing it instead of clipping it.	Sharpen rotary mowers after every two or three mowings.

3 The Landscape: Planning and Planting Your Shrubs, Trees, and Ground Covers

North American gardens and yards are products of a melting pot. Just as natives of dozens of countries have contributed to the growth and strength of both the United States and Canada, so too have they contributed their ideas—and the plants and seeds they brought with them—to the developing concepts of how to use the space around their homes, concepts molded to suit the various climates and needs of the continent. Constantly evolving over time, the gardens of today are quite different from those of earlier generations.

When you travel in England, you both expect and find, if not the actual gardens designed by Gertrude Jekyll and Edwin Lutyens, surely the formality and careful color blending that marked the work of that pair. Visit Japan, and you see the deceptively simple gardens that reflect a centuries-old art form and that demonstrate how much beauty can be created in the smallest of areas. In North America, however, there is no single garden type to be discovered. Here are carefully planned herb gardens, bountiful vegetable gardens, vast expanses of lawn, collections of plants such as daylilies or roses, fortresslike hedges, and even overgrown "foundation" plantings that threaten to shadow second-story windows—a magnificent variety of landscaping and gardening schemes all reflecting the interests, ambitions, capabilities, even ancestral backgrounds of gardeners.

◀ *Well-planned and carefully tended plantings enhance the value of any property.*

HOW TO BEGIN PLANNING YOUR OWN LANDSCAPING

Let's take a moment to mention some of the factors worth considering when we make basic landscape planning decisions.

Most of us want the growing space around our homes to be a place for family living, as well as entertaining and cooking evening and weekend meals. These purposes are well served by a patio surrounded by plantings, with areas for socializing and space for containers filled with shrubs, vegetables, and even small fruit trees. For small children, the yard is a haven, a place to enjoy and learn about the outdoors. As the children grow, it can become a gathering place for them and their friends.

Most of us, too, want a home garden that is easily maintained. We're willing—usually, if reminded—to mow a lawn weekly. In the spring, it seems as though some chemical change in our body impels us to get out there with shovel, rake, mower, and hoe, to scatter seed and fertilizer, to plant bulbs and perennials, and to prune vigorously. And for the rest of the year? Please, nothing too vigorous, and particularly nothing that has to be done daily. Remember, too, that we go away on vacation for several weeks in the summer, and, like it or not, the gardens and the lawn must take care of themselves during that time.

There are, of course, exceptions to this: the truly devoted, to whom the doing is as much a pleasure as the result. But most of us want it simple. Life has challenges enough; we have no desire to plant our own.

This attitude, perhaps surprisingly, has had a welcome effect on our gardening. In recent years, for example, we've tended away from choosing a predictable selection of foundation plantings favored by all landscapers and moved toward selecting shrubs and trees native to our own areas that fare well with little

A patio provides an outdoor space for living and entertaining.

Positive Images, Tad Goodale

help from us. This has added a refreshing divergency to our landscaping throughout the continent.

Finally, we want to be proud of our gardens and lawn. There's a purely financial reason for this. A well-planned and carefully tended garden can add thousands of dollars to the price of the house when we sell it. But this is rarely a concern unless we must move. Far more simply, we enjoy having visitors exclaim about what we have created. Perhaps even more important, we enjoy walking out of the house in the morning, or coming home to it in the evening, and smiling in satisfaction at what we see.

Our family is young and growing. How do I begin planning our yard for both beauty and function?

Whether you are designing a new landscape or improving an existing one, your first step is to define exactly what you want to accomplish. This does not mean selecting shrubs or patio furniture. Rather, you must begin by making decisions about what you want to create. Try writing down your needs and goals. Here's an example:

- Front yard should reflect the friendliness and warmth of our home, inviting our friends and neighbors to come in and join us.
- Area on right side of house should be screened in some way to eliminate eyesores in the service area, where we have tool storage and trash cans; would shrubs be better than a fence?
- Left side should be an open expanse of lawn.
- Shrubs (or beds of annual flowers?) will serve to suggest a division of the left side lawn from the rear area.
- Backyard should be an extension of our life inside the house: a place for entertaining and for evening family meals; a playing area for the children and their friends, including a sandbox now and perhaps a pool when we can afford it; space for frisbee playing and volleyball; flower and vegetable gardens—fit in as many activities as possible without having the area look crowded or allowing activities to encroach upon each other.

An open backyard with a dense growth of grass plants is ideal for games such as croquet.

Your list of goals may be far different from this example. You may want a formal public area in front of the house and a quiet place for reading and meditation in the rear. Whatever you want, get it down on paper. Listing your goals will help as you make specific decisions on such things as placement of new shrubs and trees.

How much privacy should I attempt to provide?

This really depends upon your location and the degree of privacy that you desire. You will want to wall out the noise and traffic of a busy highway; on the other hand, you may enjoy making a quiet street with beautiful residences part of your landscape. In general, unless there is a real need for privacy, it is better to share landscapes with neighbors by avoiding high hedges and fences that delineate property lines. You and your neighbors thus benefit equally from the sense of spaciousness that is created. In this way, an effort to improve landscaping at any house tends to upgrade the neighborhood and stimulates others to attempt improvements.

How can I distinguish the various areas around the house according to their uses?

First is the public area in front of your house, the area that tells people about you and your house. You can vary, of course, from these generalizations, but often the best choice for front yards is conservative—a spacious area of lawn, evergreen or deciduous shrubs to soften the foundation line, a tree or two to frame the house and provide some shade.

The service area, containing such items as vegetable garden, compost piles, and a shed for storage, can be downplayed or disguised by well-placed shrubs.

Finally, the outdoor living area should be an extension of the activities of the family in the home. A patio is often the feature point, easily accessible from the house, and placed, if possible, so it has the morning sun but is shaded in the afternoon. Too often, patios are larger than necessary. A patio should be about the same size as the rooms in your house, overly spacious only if you do a lot of large-group entertaining.

Locate other activities so they don't interfere with activities on the patio. Play areas for children should be close enough so the youngsters can be watched, either from the patio or inside the house. Remember, too, that children grow fast, and their interests change at a comparable speed. They'll soon outgrow the sandbox and the slide, so plan for these changes.

DIAGRAMMING YOUR LANDSCAPE

Whether you are landscaping your present property or studying a possible site for a new home, you need a landscape plan on paper. This takes time to draw, but it can be one of the most important moves you make. Just drawing it forces you to take a close look at your lot, and working with it enables you to make mistakes and change your mind before you plant without any cost—or, equally undesirable, the need to live with your mistakes.

What *is* a landscape plan?

It is a map of your land, showing property lines, all buildings, walks, drives, utility poles and lines, and fences or walls. It should indicate all existing trees and shrubs—including variety, height, and width—gardens, and play areas. It should also include some things that are not on your property, such as neighboring trees that shade your property and outlooks toward eyesores *or* beautiful views. If your plan is to be used to help decide the site of a house, it will need additional information, such as rock outcroppings that would complicate the placement of the foundation and any soil conditions that would influence the location for a septic system.

What is the first step toward drawing a map of my land?

To prepare for making a scale drawing, make a rough sketch of the features of your property on a sheet of paper on which you can jot down measurements later as you make them. Draw in the boundary lines first. Position the house as exactly as possi-

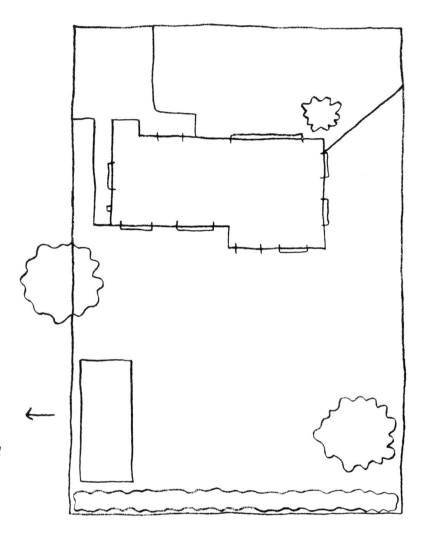

A rough sketch of your property should indicate such features as property lines, buildings, walks, drives, utility poles and lines, fences, trees and shrubs, gardens, and play areas.

ble, locating all windows, doors, and patios. Indicate the position of all objects on the property—both man-made and natural.

How do I go about making an actual scale drawing?

Depending on the size of your paper and the size of your lot, choose graph paper and establish a scale. For example, for a three-by-three-foot sheet of paper and a 100-by-100-foot lot, a scale of one-quarter inch equals one foot is good. Although a smaller sheet can be photocopied easily, thus enabling you to try out several plans on paper for comparison, it may be difficult to get adequate detail on too small a plan.

Next, take your rough drawing outdoors and make all of the measurements necessary to translate that drawing to scale on your graph paper.

When you have completed your drawing, add a North arrow and a date, then begin ''planting'' on it. If the permanent objects on your plan are outlined in black ink, you can make your ''proposals'' lightly in pencil right on the map, or you can lay a piece of tracing paper over the map and try out several different schemes.

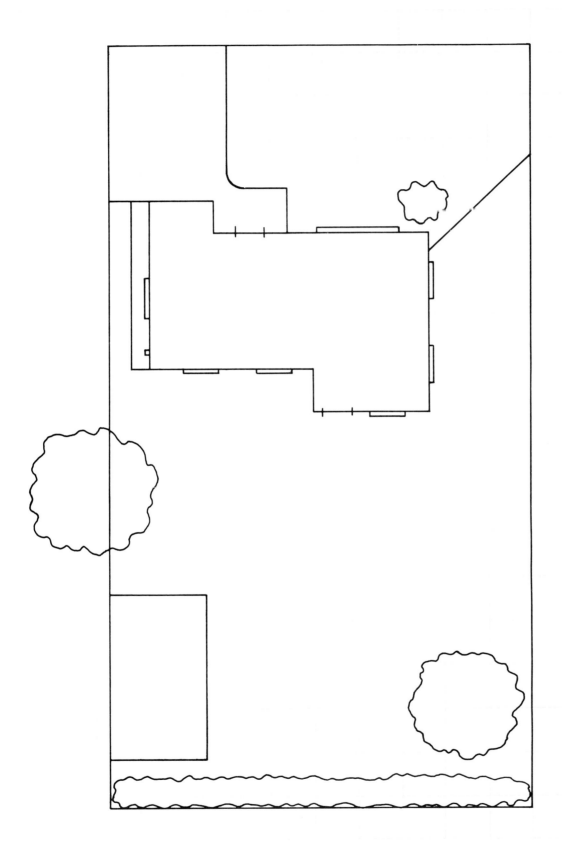

A scale drawing translates your rough sketch into an exact plan of your property.

USING YOUR LANDSCAPING PLAN

Here are some very basic thoughts to consider as you try out various arrangements on your landscaping plan:

- An unbroken lawn, bordered with shrubs and flowers, gives a good appearance. Have a valid reason before you plunk something in the center of it.
- A scattering of shrubs of various kinds looks unplanned and messy. Several of the same variety grouped together in a bed gives a unified appearance and a much stronger effect than a single shrub. If planting three or more, avoid planting them in a row.
- Foundation plantings (deciduous and evergreen shrubs planted near the house foundation) keep a home from appearing naked. There is nothing in the law that says plantings must all be small evergreens. Native plants, in particular, often make good foundation plantings. They blend in particularly well with similar plants elsewhere on the property and require very little care.
- In most cases, foundation plantings look best when taller plants are used to soften corner lines

and smaller plants are used near the main entrance door to the house.

- For plants under windows, select those that will grow no higher than the bottom of the window. Taller growing varieties may be chosen, of course, but then you should plan on annual, naturalistic pruning.
- For every shrub that you plant, have a reason, such as breaking the blankness of a wall, providing background for flower beds, suggesting divisions between various areas, or screening work or play areas.
- A tree directly in front of a house is usually a mistake. Rather, plant the tree at one side to help frame the house.
- When deciding on the location of a tree, the common error is to be guided by its size at the time it is planted, rather than by its mature size. As a result, we often see trees planted so close to a house that their branches brush against it, trees overpowering the front of a house, or large trees out of scale beside small houses.
- The first rule of planting trees is to be guided by where you do or do not want shading.

In advance of building on a lot, is there anything that can be done that would improve the land or save time later on?

Clear out undesirable trees and thick wild growth. Identify with the builder any native shrub masses that you wish to leave untouched. When the cellar hole is dug, have the topsoil saved and the soil beneath it either carried away or spread where it will not interfere with your plans. If this subsoil is dumped where you wish to plant, it will bury the valuable topsoil and make it more difficult to plant there (see pages 8–9).

We have a new home and a flat, bare lot to landscape completely, with very little money to put into it. What do you advise for first plantings to take away the bare, new look?

Shade trees come first. Bare-root trees (packaged with sphagnum moss rather than with the soil in which they grew; see page 83) are most economical, but should be planted in the early spring. Next, buy foundation plantings for the front, beginning with small, and therefore less expensive, plants. Add other shrubs and plantings as you can afford them. Not only does this spread your costs out, but if you plan carefully and buy slowly, you have a chance to evaluate and modify your plan as you see how things are coming along, and thus you may be much more satisfied with your results than if you bought and planted everything at one time.

I plan to build on a lot that's only one-hundred by fifty feet. What can I do about landscaping?

It may surprise you, but landscaping is probably more important on your lot than a larger one, simply because it's often easier to create beauty on a larger lot. You have specific and challenging conditions—little land, lack of privacy, and a need to enrich the space you have—all of which can be addressed by thoughtful landscaping. First, much can be done with the proper design and placement of the house to assure views of your lawn area that can be enjoyed from inside the house and to use as little space as possible for drives and service areas. Plan a lawn area unbroken by decorations, shrubs, or trees; it will thus appear more spacious. Don't crowd the remaining space with too many activities, such as vegetable gardens, eating areas, or flower beds. Select and concentrate on one, keeping it near the edge, rather than in the center of your lot. Finally, avoid plantings, such as hedges, on all the boundary lines of your lot. They will make the lot seem much smaller.

Will you suggest economical landscaping for a small temporary home?

Maintain extreme simplicity. Use the minimum of planting on the front and sides of the house. In the rear, if possible, plant a compact vegetable garden bordered with annual and perennial flowers.

I recently bought a 157-year-old house with overgrown shrubbery and beds, and trees shading a mossy lawn. Should I clear it all away and start fresh?

You have a challenge. In addition to buying a house, you bought the landscaping decisions, many of them poorly thought out, of generations of owners of that house. Move slowly as you improve the grounds. A tree once felled is gone forever. Shrubs, as well as trees, are expensive to buy, and many of yours probably can be salvaged by removing dead or damaged growth, then pruning them to the size you wish. And, of course, they can be moved. A thorough knowledge of the shrubs—their names, growth, and flowering habits—is essential before you make decisions on whether to retain or remove them.

Approach your challenge by drawing three plans. On one, show the lot as it is, complete with house and garage, walks and driveway, and all of that vegetation you mentioned. The second plan should show the same permanent fixtures and what you want to salvage of the natural features. You must either cut enough of those trees to introduce sunshine to your lawn and

Positive Images, Jerry Howard

Plan landscaping so that views can be enjoyed from the inside as well as outside.

An older home with many large plant-ings offers a different kind of challenge.

foundation beds, or select shade-tolerant plants. Consider the age, position (good or bad), size, and beauty of trees as you make decisions. The final plan should show how you want your landscaping to be when you've finished.

As you go out on your grounds to work, remove trees first, work with your shrubs next, and leave your lawn until last. Much as builders leave laying the carpet until last, you should work on your lawn after you have removed trees, possibly dug up old flower beds and some shrubs, and made all decisions on your layout. Have the soil tested by your Extension Service or do it yourself with a soil-testing kit available at garden centers (that moss makes me think it may be very acid; see pages 34–36), then follow the directions in the lawn section for rebuilding a lawn (pages 25-27).

My colonial house has a very plain doorway. How can I plant near it to make it seem more important?

When the doorway is formal but very plain, interest may be created through the planting. Use identical groups on either side, but select the plants carefully, striving for variety of form, texture, and color. Evergreens give great dignity and are less likely to get too large in a short time. Mass taller plants to accent the lines of the doorway, with spreading plants around them for the most effective arrangement.

We have large trees (oak, gray birch, maple, and ironwood) on our lawn. What should be planted near the house? The yard slopes toward the south and the house is new, so we are starting from scratch.

Let the trees be the principal landscape feature. Use a minimum of planting near the house. Try ground covers (see pages 85-91) along the foundation, plus a few shade-loving shrubs at the corners or at either side of the entrance.

What is the best method of foundation planting for a house with the front door off-center?

An unbalanced, or asymmetrical, composition for a foundation planting can be extremely attractive, and an off-center door will make it even more interesting. Use a variety of shrubs, both deciduous and evergreen, of different heights, colors, and textures, and be sure to include some flowering shrubs.

How shall I landscape the front of our Cape Cod home? Built about 1810, the main house features a front door in the center with an ell and a long shed-garage combination. What treatment along the front would you suggest?

Planting for a Cape Cod house should be very simple. A formal fountain, for example, would attract attention because of its inappropriateness. Consider a boxwood, privet (pruned to a

Here an asymmetrical garden by the front door provides an understated and effective foundation planting.

rounded form), or Japanese holly on each side of the door, and clumps of lilacs at each corner of the house. Many old homes traditionally have two shade trees in the front lawn, one on each side of the door. A small dooryard garden enclosed by a low picket fence would also be charming.

The central doorway of my house is a reproduction of an old colonial door, with leaded side lights and a fanlight. How should I plant around this so as to enhance rather than detract from its beauty?

For an elaborate doorway, complicated planting is unnecessary. Possibly the most effective thing would be to plant a large lilac on either side of the door. For a more formal effect, plant an Irish or cone-shaped yew on either side.

What sort of foundation planting is appropriate for a French chateau-type house?

French architecture calls for a formal style of planting. Hold the plantings to a minimum, using evergreens, such as yew, boxwood, euonymus, and holly, clipped into formal shapes.

I live on the ground floor of a small apartment house and thus have the use of a small (sixteen-by-sixteen-foot) walled-in area behind the house that I would like to use. What can I do? The area gets sunshine all afternoon, but the soil looks worthless.

You can create an outside room in that area that will give you space to garden and to entertain, and possibly provide a pleas-

Symmetrical and simple plantings are most suitable for a plain but formal entrance door.

For a new house, concentrate on placing suitable trees; use low-growing ground covers near the foundation.

ant scene from inside your apartment as well. Along the sides of your area, in both shaded and sunny spots, create a few raised beds framed by lumber or bricks and filled with three or four inches of good soil. Pave most of the rest of the area with bricks or flagstones on which to place a few lawn chairs and a table. Choose furniture of a muted color so it doesn't dominate your space. Paint the walls either a light shade or white; the reflected light will improve lighting in the area. Consider growing flowers, vegetables, and even fruits in large pots or other containers.

Choose your plants carefully. Many kinds of flowers will flourish in the sun, of course, but there are quite a few varieties, such as impatiens and begonias, that will do well in shady spots. Also consider planting ground covers, such as ground ivy or periwinkle.

Vines, either annual or perennial (see pages 121–122), will do well under the conditions you have described, and if trained on trellises or other structures, will add interest to your wall areas. You can provide more privacy for your outdoor room by erecting an overhead trellis to support the vines.

Your trees and shrubs are the backbone of your landscaping plan. They frame the house, provide an appealing background for flowers and other focal points, screen objectionable views, and provide shade, protection from the wind, and privacy. If selected and placed intelligently, they create a beautiful setting that is of colorful interest every month of the year, guaranteeing a home landscape that will provide you and others great pleasure.

For an inexperienced gardener like myself, the increasingly varied selection of specimens available at nurseries makes choices difficult. I know I want to plant a crab apple tree, but which of the hundreds available should I select? I like lilacs, mock-oranges, and other plants, too, and they offer the same bewildering number of choices.

Begin by identifying where you need plants. Then study the conditions for their growth and look for the best plants to fit your needs. If there is any buying trend today, it's toward smaller trees and shrubs—the ten-foot crab apple, for example, instead of the 100-foot oak. Consumers are learning to select with future needs in mind. If your home and grounds are small, instead of choosing a tiny lilac and finding yourself with a fifteen- or twenty-foot tall shrub years later, select a Dwarf Snowflake or some other lilac that reaches three feet in height—and remains there. Select trees and shrubs that grow well in your local conditions so that you won't have to fuss with something that will never acclimatize to your area.

Would it be better to select a landscape architect to design our property?

You may decide to hire a landscape architect or designer to advise you in plant selection. This person can make all of the decisions for you, based on your description of hoped-for results. He or she may even purchase and plant your shrubs and trees, and start to revive a lawn. This, of course, can be expensive, sometimes leaving you with little more satisfaction than writing a check.

I have never gardened before and my first trip to my local nursery was rather overwhelming. How do I know where to begin?

Neophytes are often made most clearly aware of their own ignorance about gardening on their first expedition to a nursery or garden center. Where others see handsome arrays of annual and perennial plants begging to be bought and carried home, new gardeners see only questions. Is my soil right for that one? Will that one grow in the shade? And this tree—how high will it grow, and how wide? If beginners walk away in dismay, or make a purchase just to have something to plant, they're miss-

CHOOSING YOUR PLANTINGS

ing out on one of the biggest bargains around: free information from nursery personnel. They want you, not merely as a customer, but as a satisfied customer, returning year after year as you improve the landscaping at your home. They know from bitter experience that if they sell you the healthiest of plants and it dies under the less than tender—although possibly very loving—care you provide, they've lost a customer, since you inevitably perceive the failure to be theirs and not yours.

Perhaps I would be better off saving money at a discount store?

You can, of course, save money by going to a discount store for your plants and supplies, but this can be dangerous unless you're knowledgeable. The plants shipped to these stores may not be the best for your geographical area, and they may not have received the best of care since being put out for sale. Further, you are unlikely to get informed advice on the planting and care of what you buy.

What are the advantages of depending on a garden center for my needs?

In most cases, a good nursery or garden center is the best source for beginners, in particular. They've carefully selected the best plants for your area, they've treated them like the babes some of them are, and they will charge you nothing for the information they dispense with every sale. They have one thing in common, however: In return for picking their brains, you're expected to buy at their shops.

How do I set up an effective relationship with a good garden center?

Garden centers have two methods for giving information to customers with numerous questions. Some will visit your home, talk with you, and then submit a plan showing their recommendations for purchases and where those purchases should be placed. More commonly, nursery personnel expect you to map your lot, then discuss it with them at the nursery. The advantage of this method is that they can show you the recommended plants. However they work, nursery personnel recognize that in most cases money for landscaping is limited, so they will suggest a planting schedule that extends over several years.

Get the most out of free assistance by some thoughtful preparation. First, schedule a convenient time to visit your garden center, preferably in advance of the season. Don't drop in on a spring Saturday morning when nurseries do the largest volume of their year's business. Understandably, those weekends are times for nurseries to take in cash and move to the next customer. Instead, call long before the season opens and set a time that's mutually convenient. Give them a hint of what help you want.

Next, before your meeting, make a sketch of your lot and take a few color photos of your house from different viewpoints. Be prepared to answer some basic questions about your property. Any rocky areas? Wet areas? Steep banks or hills? Is the soil sandy, clay, or good loam? You might take along a soil sample. It's often easier to show than to tell.

Expect to tell something about yourself. The person helping you will probably grasp quickly the depth of your gardening knowledge but will want to know if you're willing to do a lot of work or prefer landscaping that is nearly maintenance-free. You must also give a hint of how much you are willing to spend. Much can be done to move costs up and down, through suggestions of specific plants, as well as selection of younger and thus less expensive plants.

Given all this information, most nursery personnel will not only recommend purchases to you, but tell you where they will do best, when and how they should be planted, and how you should care for them. This can be the start of a profitable relationship for both of you.

One of the first questions I faced at my garden center was whether I was interested in deciduous or evergreen trees and shrubs. What is the difference?

Deciduous plants lose most or all of their leaves yearly; evergreen plants have foliage that stays green and functional through more than one growing season.

What do you consider some of the most handsome and functional shrubs for home landscapes, and what are their basic traits?

Endless information about specific varieties is available in books, arboretums and botanical gardens, nurseries and garden centers. The list of shrubs on page 75 provides a solid beginning catalogue of fine shrubs, but you will soon find that there are thousands of plants available to today's landscaper.

How could a rather steep, partly wooded hillside be planted to make it more attractive?

A wooded hillside can be underplanted with native shrubs, such as mountain laurel, azaleas, and rhododendrons, along with ferns and woodland wildflowers. A system of trails leading through the area would add to its interest.

What is best for planting around a small house on a small acreage? Everyone has evergreens. Can't we be different?

Deciduous shrubs can be just as interesting throughout much of the year, although evergreens are more apt to lend interest and color in the winter. An all-deciduous planting, however,

SHRUBS

Positive Images, Jerry Howard

Native shrubs, ground covers, and a handsome stone walkway invite browsers to explore this wooded hillside.

Positive Images, Jerry Howard

Azaleas and rhododendrons usher in spring with floods of color.

can certainly work well. Another possibility is to use deciduous shrubs with a few evergreens as a background.

What sort of shrubbery would you plant in front of a new house with a thirty-foot frontage?

Avoid too much planting. If the house foundation is low enough, leave some spaces bare to show the house standing solidly on the ground. Both deciduous and evergreen plantings are suitable, and a variety of colors and textures is most effective. Cypress, yews, azaleas, rhododendrons, and boxwood are only some of the many popular choices.

What plants should be used around a modern ranch-type house in front of a large rock outcrop?

By all means, make use of the natural rock, planting rock plants and creeping junipers around it. Low yews and azaleas might be in the foundation planting, with a dogwood or crab apples at the corners or off to the side.

Will you suggest some shrubs for the rocky bank in front of our house?

Junipers are always good, both bush form and trailing types for over the rocks. Memorial rose, *Crispa stephanandra*, and Arnold Dwarf forsythia all root wherever their branches touch the soil, and they are ideal for such situations. If vines would qualify, try climbing hydrangea, English ivy, or Virginia creeper.

SELECTED SHRUBS

AUTUMN SAGE, *Salvia Greggii*. Popular in the Southwest, this woody perennial grows three feet high, is drought-resistant, and has clusters of red to purple flowers in fall.

AZALEA, *Rhododendron*. There are many kinds of azalea, both deciduous and evergreen, so that in almost every part of North America you should be able to grow this popular shrub. Most common varieties grow three to six feet high and are among the most brilliant of the flowering shrubs. Many bloom before the leaves are formed. They grow both in shade and filtered sunlight and require ample moisture.

BLUE SPIREA, *Caryopteris incana* (zone 7 south*). These low plants are useful for borders. They have showy blue flowers in fall.

BOXWOOD, *Buxus sempervirens* (zone 6 south). Boxwood does particularly well in Maryland and Virginia. Boxwoods range from dwarfs to twenty-five-foot-tall trees, often pruned to formal shapes. They need acid soil and ample moisture.

CAMELLIA, *Camellia japonica* (zone 8). Particularly popular in the South Atlantic states, this shrub is sometimes seen as a tree up to twenty-five feet tall. The many varieties are all prized for their showy blooms. Most require acid soil and good drainage.

CORAL ARDISIA, *Ardisia crispa* (zones 9 and 10). This foot-high evergreen has white flowers in the spring and red berries in the fall and winter.

CRAPE MYRTLE, *Lagerstroemia indica* (zone 7 south). This shrub can grow to a twenty-foot tree. Its pink blossoms are a late summer attraction. Although it can be grown from seed, its flowers aren't always true to the color of the plant from which the seed was taken; it may also be propagated by cuttings.

FORSYTHIA, *Forsythia intermedia* (zones 5 to 8). Forsythia grows six to eight feet high and is noted for its brilliant yellow flowers early in the spring.

HONEYSUCKLE, *Lonicera tatarica* (zones 3 to 9). Bush (common) honeysuckle grows up to ten feet tall and, depending on the variety, has white to pink blossoms in spring.

HYDRANGEA, *Hydrangea macrophylla* (zones 5 to 9). This shrub usually grows three to four feet tall, though it can reach twelve feet. It has beautiful blue or pink flower clusters in midsummer.

LILAC, *Syringa*. A variety of lilac can be found for every zone except 10. One of the most popular

*Zone map appears on page 138.

shrubs, lilacs originally were always purple, but now colors range from white, pink, and blue to deep purple.

MOCK ORANGE, *Philadelphus coronarius* (zones 4 to 9). Mock orange grows about seven feet tall. This well-loved, old-fashioned shrub bears fragrant white flowers in late spring.

MOUNTAIN LAUREL, *Kalmia latifolia* (zones 4 to 9). This handsome shrub has large rose and white flower clusters in early summer. It grows well in shady areas with acid soil. It should be massed for greatest effect.

Positive Images, Jerry Howard

Blue-flowering hydrangea is an old-fashioned and dependable favorite.

OREGON GRAPE HOLLY, *Mahonia Aquifolium* (zones 5 to 8). Oregon grape holly does well in shade. It has fragrant yellow flowers in spring, interesting blue fruit in summer, and is particularly beautiful in fall, when its foliage turns red.

RHODODENDRON, *Rhododendron* (zones 5 to 8). Most rhododendrons today are evergreen hybrid shrubs with white, pink, red, or purple blooms. They require rich, acid soil, ample moisture, and some shade.

ROSE OF SHARON, *Hibiscus syriacus* (zones 5 to 9). Rose of Sharon grows six to eight feet high and is noted for its brilliant yellow flowers early in the spring.

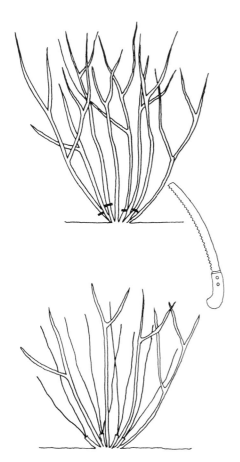

(Top) with a small saw, cut the largest stems down at ground level; (bottom) new growth will spring from the pruned branches to create a fuller shrub.

Please name a few evergreen shrubs that do well in light shade.

Abelia, barberry, mahonia, mountain laurel, leucothoe, privet, andromeda (*Pieris*), rhododendron, evergreen azalea, yew, arborvitae, and certain viburnums.

Can shrubs and small trees be used in a flower garden?

Yes, an occasional compact-growing tree or shrub in the garden relieves the monotony of perennial and annual plantings. The tree rose is especially suitable.

We plan to landscape a three-acre tract. Will you name some plants that give a succession of color throughout the year?

For spring, use azalea, forsythia, rhododendron, or spicebush viburnum. For summer, use honeysuckle, hydrangea, buddleia, roses, heather, or rose of Sharon. For fall flowers use abelia or witch hazel. For fall foliage color use *Euonymus alatus*, dogwood, enkianthus, viburnum, Japanese barberry, sumac, spicebush, and blueberry.

We have a huge, overgrown lilac. Although it is beautiful in the spring when it is covered with blossoms, it is far too large for its location. What can we do?

Using a small saw, so you won't injure the other stems, cut down at ground level the largest stems until those remaining are the height you want. This will not damage the plant. When doing this, however, don't prune the branches you wish to keep, as you might with other shrubs, or you may cut away next season's blossoms.

Maggie Oster

A variety of colors and textures of deciduous trees and shrubs, ground covers, and vines makes this an attractive nook, even without flowers.

What are some considerations to keep in mind when choosing trees?

Select trees based on their usage: shade, wind protection, ornament, or food production. In a setting near a home, the height of the mature tree is important. Many fine shade trees reach a height of 100 feet or more, excellent in a roomy setting, but far too large for smaller lots. Our list of trees contains many that are of moderate mature height and are thus suitable for the smaller home lot. Equally important, be certain the trees you choose grow well in your area. Since there are several hundred varieties of trees, our list (pages 77-78) is only a representative selection.

I have an area where I would like to have some shade as soon as possible. I know that poplars grow quickly. Would they be a good choice?

Think of poplars as a last resort if nothing else will grow in the area. The small branches that continuously fall from poplars make them messy trees. Furthermore, their spreading roots often plug drains or other pipes. Their virtues, on the other hand, are that they will grow in damp areas and they do reach full growth in a few years. A better choice, nevertheless, is one of the faster-growing maples, which will add beauty as well as shade to your area, without the disadvantages of poplars.

How do I provide shade for the patio?

Plant a dogwood, crab apple, magnolia, or some other small tree. Dogwood, in particular, is ideal because its horizontal branching habit allows one to sit under it.

TREES

Positive Images, Jerry Howard

This maple shows its early spring color.

SELECTED SHADE TREES

GINKGO, *Ginkgo biloba* (zone 5 south*). Ginkgo is also known as the maidenhair tree. Because female trees have a foul-smelling fruit, plant only the male trees. Young trees have irregular branches, but they eventually fill out. They can grow to more than 100 feet in height. Because of their hardiness, they are excellent for the stressful conditions along streets.

MOUNTAIN ASH, *Sorbus aucuparia* (zones 3 to 9). Mountain ash grows to about thirty feet high. It will tolerate some shade and dry soil. Its natural beauty is enhanced by white flower clusters in the spring, followed by bunches of orange-scarlet berries. This showy tree is a good selection when you want to feature a tree as a focal point.

PIN OAK, *Quercus palustris* (zones 5 to 8). Pin oak

*Zone map appears on page 138.

will reach seventy-five feet in height. Its leaves turn red in fall. It is an excellent choice for a large lawn. There are some 200 other species of oaks, most of which grow to be large trees. Many of them, native to specific areas, are excellent choices for roomy grounds.

SUGAR MAPLE, *Acer saccharum* (zones 4 to 8). This slow-growing tree will reach 100 or more feet when it is mature. Along with many of the other maples it is an excellent shade tree and suitable for street plantings. Smaller maples, such as *A. ginnala*, *A. palmatum*, and *A. tataricum*, grow only twenty to thirty feet high, so they bring the easy grace of the maple to smaller home grounds without dominating the landscape.

SELECTED ORNAMENTAL TREES

FLOWERING CRAB APPLE, *Malus* (all zones except the deep South*). There are many varieties and hybrids of flowering crab apple. All are early bloomers, and many grow only fifteen feet, with few more than thirty feet high. Many have showy fruit in the fall and winter.

FLOWERING AND KOUSA DOGWOODS, *Cornus florida* and *C. Kousa* (zones 5 to 9). This is one of the most popular of the flowering trees, with white, pink, or red flowers in early spring; the foliage is scarlet in fall. Dogwood's maximum height is thirty feet.

FLOWERING CHERRY, *Prunus serrulata*, *P. Subhirtella*, and *P. yedoensis* (zones 5 to 9). Flowering cherry grows from twelve to thirty feet tall. To show these trees off the best, plant them about twenty-five feet apart. They need sun, good drainage, and rich soil to achieve their peak blooms during early spring.

The famous cherry trees in Washington, D.C., usually bloom in early April.

MAGNOLIA, *Magnolia* (best in zones 5 to 9). Some magnolias produce their handsome flowers before the foliage; some come into bloom and put out leaves at the same time. Magnolia is available in shrubs as well as trees, some reaching thirty feet in height.

WEEPING BIRCH, *Betula pendula laciniata* (zones 3 to 8). The finely cut leaves of this white-barked birch turn yellow in the fall. It grows to about thirty feet in height. Consider as well, other white-barked birches, such as clump birch, with several trunks growing together to a height of about twenty-five feet; the large (up to ninety feet) canoe, or paper, birch; and European white birch, which is smaller than canoe birch.

Positive Images, Jerry Howard

Positive Images, Jerry Howard

Flowering crab apple is heavily laden with deep pink flowers in early spring.

*Zone map appears on page 138.

Flowering white dogwood with its horizontal branches is an ideal tree to use near houses.

FRUIT TREES

I've always wanted to grow fruit trees, but I have neither much space nor much knowledge. Have you any advice?

One of the finest advances for amateur gardeners who wish to grow fruit trees has been the development of dwarf trees. This, combined with the development of easy-to-follow programs of disease and insect control, now makes it possible to have a productive family orchard, complete with fruit trees, berry bushes, and grape vines, in a space as small as fifty by fifty feet.

What must I consider before I plant fruit trees?

• First consult your family about their likes and dislikes.

Positive Images, Jerry Howard

The pleasures of growing fruit trees are possible even on properties with limited space.

- Understand the pollination habits of each tree. Some fruit trees, such as peaches and apricots, are self-compatible, which means they can make use of their own pollen in order to bear fruit. Others, such as many apples, sweet cherries, and pears, require another variety of the same fruit to be blossoming nearby at the same time.
- Ascertain the area required for each tree, so you can plan your orchard properly. Available trees range from standard (with thirty-five feet between trees) to semidwarf (twelve to eighteen feet between trees), dwarf (ten to twelve feet between trees), and even extra-dwarf, which grow only seven feet tall and can be planted as closely together as six feet.
- Lay your orchard out in a sunny, well-drained area with rich soil.
- Carry out a program of pruning and spraying at the recommended times.

I have an area where I wish to plant several fruit trees. It is extremely sandy. Will it help if I place a layer of topsoil over the area?

The topsoil, tilled in, would aid you in establishing a grass crop around the trees. But to help the trees, it's necessary to get the better soil down around the root areas.

Dig large holes, taking out at least a bushel of sand from each one. Make a mix of half topsoil and half compost or other organic matter. Put enough of this in the hole so that when the tree is planted it will be at the level it was growing previously. Put the

A standard apple tree is eminently suitable for home landscapes.

tree in the hole, hold it straight, and cover the roots with several inches of soil mix. Fill the hole with water and wait until the water has drained away. Then fill the hole with the mix and firm the soil well in around the root area.

What is the best way to prepare heavy clay for fruit trees?

The greatest danger you face is that drainage may be poor and thus water will stand around the tree roots, requiring installation of a drainage system. If you decide this is not necessary, try to improve the soil by working in a quantity of organic material. Instead of returning the clay soil to the hole when planting the tree, substitute topsoil.

When should I prune my fruit trees?

Any time between harvest and the beginning of spring growth—in other words, late fall to late winter, the dormant, or resting period. Preventive spraying is also beneficial at this time.

I've just lost another fruit tree to mice girdling it. What can I do? It seems to happen every winter.

Just a few mice can cause an impressive amount of damage around a house. They not only injure trees but feed on bulbs as well. Trees can be protected two ways. One is to wind the lower part of the trunk with a plastic wrapping sold expressly for this purpose; or place a strip of quarter-inch metal mesh around the

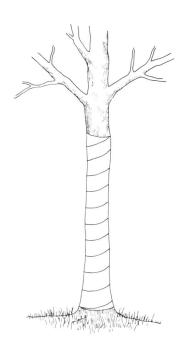

Protective plastic wrapping discourages small animals from nibbling the bark of young trees.

80

tree, wide enough so it extends firmly down into the soil and at least a foot up the trunk. In the fall, remove any leaf or hay mulches, which are probably living quarters for the mice. A hungry cat provides the best long-term protection.

Tape wrapping will also keep the sun and winds from drying out and cracking the bark.

PLANTING SHRUBS AND TREES

It seems so simple: Buy a tree or shrub, take it home, dig a hole, and plant it. While it can be that easy, the beginner should know that one error in the process can mean that the plant may take as many as three years to return to health, or it may not even survive the transplanting. The process of transplanting begins with selection of the plant and doesn't end until that plant is in the ground and, if necessary, held in place with stakes.

When is the best time to plant trees?

For most trees and shrubs, the planting time isn't that critical. While spring and fall are best for most plants, many of them, especially balled-and-burlapped or container-grown stock (see definitions below) can be planted during most of the growing season, since their roots will not be disturbed during planting. Bare-root plants, however, should go into the ground in the very early spring while they are still dormant.

What are bare-root plants? Are there special techniques involved in planting them?

Mail-order nurseries usually ship plants *bare-root*, with the roots covered with damp sphagnum moss or some similar material. If this covering is dry when the plants are received, the roots should be soaked in water for a few minutes. Don't leave them in water if you must delay planting them for several days; that's far too much of a good thing. Bare-root plants are the easiest to damage. Extreme care must be taken, particularly when placing them in a hole, because leaving their bare roots exposed to the sun for only a few minutes can spell their end. Plant them in the spring, before any new shoots are more than three inches long, or in the autumn, after their leaves have fallen.

Please explain what *balled-and-burlapped* means.

Balled-and-burlapped trees and shrubs have been dug carefully, with the soil around their roots maintained, wrapped in burlap, and tied. A plant with a one-inch stem should have a root ball at least a foot in diameter. The most important care for balled-and-burlapped plants is to keep the root ball moist. Handled properly, the roots should be undisturbed from the time they are wrapped until they are back in the ground.

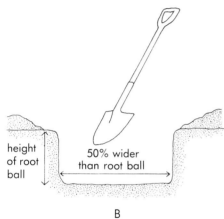

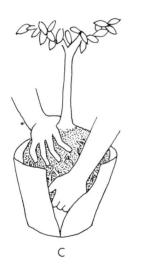

(A) Water container plants before planting; (B) dig a hole at least half again as wide as, but only slightly deeper than, the root ball; (C) cut the container if possible and remove the plant carefully, disturbing the root ball as little as necessary.

What does the term *balled-in-peat* mean?

This is a less common method, which involves digging up the plants bare-root and storing them in the late fall. In late winter or early spring, peat or other materials are placed around the roots, which are then wrapped in burlap.

What does the term *dug-and-potted* mean?

Dug-and-potted plants have been dug, bare-root, out of their nursery beds, then put into containers only a few weeks before going on sale. Thus, they've undergone stress and will undergo more when they are planted.

What are *container-grown plants?*

Container-grown plants have been grown in containers for all or most of their lives. They have the most complete and undisturbed root system.

Which packaging method offers the best chance for successful transplanting?

Container-grown or balled-and-burlapped plants.

What should I look for at the nursery when I am selecting plants?

Check for signs of mistreatment, such as broken branches, scarred or torn bark, and dry or discolored leaves. Don't buy such plants. And don't mistreat those you buy. As you carry them home, avoid slamming the stems or trunks against the side of your vehicle, ripping the root ball, or subjecting the leaves to a windy ride that will dry them out. A station wagon, rather than a pickup truck, is preferable for this trip.

Now that I have my plant home, what do I do next?

Put your tree or shrub in the shade while you dig the hole.

There are many rules for equating a plant with the size hole that's needed for it, but our recommendation is to make it wide, but not too deep. When you place the plant in the hole it should stand only slightly lower than the height at which it was originally growing. Older methods of planting suggested digging six or eight inches deeper than this so that soil enrichments could be placed in the bottom of the hole before setting the plant, but this often resulted in the plant's settling in too low after a period of time. If you have a bare-root plant, dig the hole wide enough so the roots can be spread out without crowding them. For a balled or container plant, make the hole at least half again as wide as the root ball to allow ample space at the sides to provide the plant with a rich soil mixture.

As you dig, save the topsoil and take away the subsoil. Mix enough soil enrichment to the topsoil to fill the hole. One

(Within figure B labels:) height of root ball — 50% wider than root ball

popular mixture is half topsoil and half organic matter, such as peat moss, leaf mold, or well-rotted manure. Add a half-cup of superphosphate and, if the topsoil is acid, a half-cup of lime per bushel of the topsoil-organic material mix.

Work some of this material down into the subsoil at the bottom of the hole. Then shovel in enough so the plant will be at its former growing level. Be sure to pack it firmly, adding more if necessary.

How do I treat a bare-root plant?

Heap some soil mixture in the center of the hole, so the roots will spread out and down, the way they grew. Again, be sure it is firmly packed so that there will be soil contact all around the roots and a minimum risk of settling.

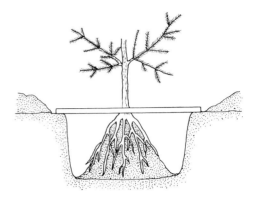

Carefully arrange the roots of bare-root plants over a mound of enriched soil; be sure plant will stand at the height it was originally planted.

What do I do with balled-and-burlapped or balled-in-peat plants? My garden center advises that I don't need to take the burlap off when I plant the shrubs. Is this right?

It is. The important thing in planting balled-and-burlapped shrubs is to avoid breaking or damaging the root ball. After you've dug a hole for a shrub, firm back into the hole enough enriched soil so the plant will stand at exactly its original height. Set the shrub in the hole, burlap and all, and add soil to about half the depth of the root ball. Then cut and remove the cord holding the burlap up to the stem. Pull the burlap away from the stem, being careful not to break the root ball. Complete filling the hole with the soil mixture. The burlap will rot away very quickly. The plastic part of plastic-reinforced burlap will not rot away, so cut away and remove it, being careful not to damage the root ball.

Unwrap about the top third of a balled-and-burlapped tree or shrub after placing it in the ground.

May plants be left in containers and planted?

Take plants out of containers before planting, even if the directions say they can be planted without doing this. These containers often restrict root penetration, which slows the growth of the plant. Take care in removing them, trying not to break the soil around the roots.

What are the final steps?

After placing the plant at the proper height, fill around it with the soil mix, making certain it doesn't settle to a lower level than it grew. The soil should be packed gently but very firmly.

With some of the remaining soil, build a small dam around the plant, out at the edges of the hole. Then water well. From five to fifteen gallons are needed to wet the soil mixture and settle it to remove air pockets. Water again a half hour later. Weekly waterings for the rest of the season are recommended; water more frequently in dry seasons.

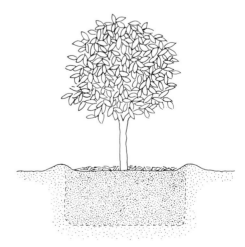

All shrubs and trees should be planted at the same depth as they originally grew. A light mulch keeps weeds down and moisture in.

I've heard I should prune trees and shrubs when I plant them. Is this true?

Pruning at planting time is no longer recommended. There are two exceptions: bare-root plants and plants you dig yourself to move to another spot. In these cases you may wish to prune in order to reduce the water requirements during the first season when roots, and particularly damaged roots, may not yet be able to furnish enough. Aim at removing from one-fourth to one-third of the leaves. First, cut away unsightly or damaged branches (but not the leader, the primary shoot), then cut back other selected branches to a lateral branch or bud. Alternatively, if you want to avoid pruning, be sure to keep the plant well watered throughout the first season, and feed it with a liquid fertilizer at half strength once a week.

Do you recommend bark mulches for newly planted trees and shrubs?

Yes, a four- to six-inch-deep layer of bark mulch is easy to apply, gives a natural, woodsy appearance, will last for several years, discourages weeds, conserves moisture, helps prevent severe freezing of roots in winter, and is easy to mow around. Begin six inches from the stem or trunk and extend the mulch to beyond the edge of the hole.

Many types of bark mulch are now available, and they have multiple uses around the yard. You'll find nuggets (three-quarters to one and one-half inches in size), larger chunks (one and one-half to three and one-half inches), shreds (stringy pieces about the size of the chunks), or chips (one-quarter- to three-quarter-inch pieces). You can also buy soil conditioner, which is dark brown and very fine in texture. It is used as a topdressing for lawns and for soil improvement in gardens and flower beds. It often has fertilizers added.

Are there materials other than bark chips that are suitable mulches?

Wood chips or pine needles are some of the materials you can use.

Do newly planted trees and shrubs require staking?

Most shrubs and small evergreen trees don't require staking, but small trees usually do, and all plants will benefit if they are apt to face high winds. The reason for staking small trees is not to prevent them from blowing over; rather, the constant force of a wind may rock the tree and loosen the small feeding roots, thus preventing the tree from becoming established.

For trees up to five feet in height, two stakes may be used. They should be hammered eighteen inches into the soil (be sure to avoid the root ball) and placed so the tree is between them. The stakes should stand high enough so that a wire can be

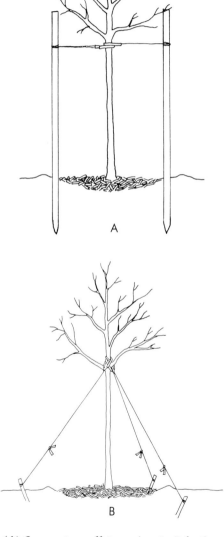

(A) Support small trees (up to 5 feet) with two wires two-thirds of the way up the tree, stretched between two stakes driven about 18 inches into the ground; (B) larger trees should be supported by 3 guy wires extending from about two-thirds of the way up the tree out to stakes about 18 inches from the tree trunk.

stretched level and reach two-thirds of the way up the tree. Cover the wire, where it touches the tree, with a section of hose. The wire should be firm, but not so tight that it pulls hard on the tree. Remove this support after a year.

To steady larger trees, use three guy wires reaching about two-thirds of the way up the tree and extending down to stakes set in the ground about eighteen inches from the trunk. Again, use sections of hose to protect the trunk. Remove the guy wires after a year.

Ground covers are low-growing plants that can be used in the following ways:

- To cover areas that are difficult to mow.
- To cover bare areas, where grass and many plants simply won't grow.
- To protect slopes where erosion is a problem.
- To add interest to lawn and garden areas.
- To guide foot traffic if used as edging along paths.

Because of the many different kinds of ground covers, one can certainly be found that is ideal for your need and that will grow well in the climate in your particular part of the country, but the variety of desirable ground covers is so great that making a final decision can prove difficult.

As a guide, consider your answers to the following questions. Is your area sunny or shady? Level or sloped? Is your soil acid or alkaline? Sand or clay? Fairly dry or usually damp? What is your plant hardiness zone? Do you want a large or small ground cover? One that is green year-round? Should it serve some additional purpose, such as providing food for birds? Your answers to these questions will determine your final choices.

What are some of your favorite ground covers?

Our list (pages 86-87) is a representative selection of ground covers suggested by the U.S. Department of Agriculture. These are among those most commonly grown. The list should be considered only as a source of suggestions, not as a limiting factor when you make your choices. All are perennials. Study also the listings for shrubs (page 75) and perennials (page 95), which often can be used with the smaller ground covers.

When should I plant ground covers?

The best time to plant in most areas is early spring; this gives the plants a chance to become well established before winter. In all cases, the soil should be prepared as for lawns by adding fertilizer and organic matter such as compost, tilling the soil, then raking it.

GROUND COVERS

·

Positive Images, Gary Mottau

Several varieties of thyme produce pleasing color and texture contrasts.

SELECTED GROUND COVERS

BEARBERRY, *Arctostaphylos Uva-ursi* (zones 2 to 9*). This fine-textured, broad-leaved evergreen grows six to ten inches high, with trailing stems, lustrous, dark foliage that turns bronze in winter, and bright red fruit. The stem may reach five to six feet in length and roots at the joints to form large clumps. It is excellent for stony, sandy, or acid soils, growing fairly well in sandy banks. It is difficult to transplant, so should be obtained as a sod or as a pot-grown plant. Some people transplant bearberry by digging up frozen clumps, then placing those in a prepared bed of sandy, acid soil.

BUGLEWEED, *Ajuga reptans* (zones 5 to 9). This creeping perennial is four to eight inches tall. It thrives in either sun or shade, grows rapidly, and tolerates most soils. It has purple leaves and dark blue flowers. Bugleweed can escape from cultivated beds and show its strength by crowding out other plants. It is, in fact, a good candidate for places where little else will grow. Propagate by seed or division.

CAPEWEED, *Lippia nodiflora* (zones 9 and 10). Also called phyla, capeweed is a creeping perennial, two to four inches in height, often used as a grass substitute. It spreads rapidly and grows in sun or shade. It can be walked on and mowed, and is more drought-resistant than many lawn grasses. Plants can be set about two feet apart. Propagate by planting sod pieces or making stem cuttings.

COTONEASTER, *Cotoneaster adpressus*, and *C. apiculatus* (zones 5 to 9), *C. Dammeri* and *C. horizontalis* (zones 6 to 10), and *C. microphyllus* (zones 7 to 10). There are more than fifty species of cotoneasters. These five are flat, horizontal-growing plants, six to thirty inches high, with bright red berries. They make excellent ground covers, particularly on banks and in rough areas. While they can't be walked on, they do seem to thrive despite neglect. *C. apiculatus* is the hardiest of this group. All do best in full sun and are attractive as accent plants with other ground covers. Cotoneasters are self-seeding, or propagate them by making cuttings.

COWBERRY, *Vaccinium Vitis-idaea* (zones 5 to 9). Also called red whortleberry, foxberry, lingonberry, and mountain cranberry, this evergreen shrub grows twelve inches high and makes an excellent ground cover in acid soils in regions with cool, moist weather in summer. Cowberry grows slowly. Propagate by dividing, making cuttings, or layering (rooting a branch by burying it in the soil, with only the tip protruding).

CREEPING LILY TURF, *Liriope spicata* (zones 5 to 10). This grasslike, evergreen perennial grows to twelve

*Zone map appears on page 138.

inches tall, and does well in hot, dry conditions, sun, or deep shade. The leaves are dark green, and the flowers range from white to purple. It can stand exposure to salt spray without injury. Once established, it forms dense growth from which small divisions can be removed for propagation.

CREEPING THYME, *Thymus Serpyllum* (zones 5 to 10). This is an evergreen species of thyme that bears purplish flowers, has pleasingly aromatic foliage, is often used as an edging or between stepping stones, and is popular in rock gardens. It rarely grows more than three inches in height, tolerates dry soils and full sun, and is a good substitute for grass in small areas. Propagate by dividing.

Periwinkle.

CROWN VETCH, *Coronilla varia* (zones 3 to 7). This is used frequently to cover dry, steep slopes. It grows one to two feet tall, and has small, pink flowers. Crown vetch spreads by underground stems, and a single plant can cover up to six feet in all directions. It prefers neutral soil but will tolerate slightly acid conditions. Propagate with cuttings. For large areas, sow seed at the rate of twenty pounds per acre. Seed should have been *scarified* (the seed coat filed or cut) to improve germination and inoculated to introduce bacteria for nitrogen fixation.

DICHONDRA, *Dichondra repens* (zones 9 and 10). This plant has runnerlike stems that spread rapidly. It seldom grows more than one or two inches tall and rarely needs clipping, so it is a favorite for lawns in the desert areas of California and other arid regions. Its enemies are winter cold and poor drainage. Propagate by replanting small clumps.

DWARF LILY TURF, *Ophiopogon japonicus* (zones 7 to 10). Also known as mondo and mondo grass, dwarf lily turf forms clumps of growth ten inches tall. It does best in moist, shaded areas.

ENGLISH IVY, *Hedera Helix* (zones 5 to 9). This popular ivy grows six to eight inches tall and forms a dense cover. Although it grows in both sun and shade, it does best in shade. Often it is planted so that it spreads across the ground, then climbs a wall. Propagate by pulling vines free and allowing them to root in a new site. Cuttings also can be started in sandy soil, then transplanted.

GERMANDER, *Teucrium Chamaedrys* (zones 6 to 10). Also known as wall germander, this woody perennial grows to ten inches tall and makes a fine border for walks. It grows well in sun or partial shade. A winter mulch may be needed where the ground freezes. Propagate by dividing or making cuttings.

GOLDMOSS STONECROP, *Sedum acre* (zones 4 to 10). This low evergreen is a good ground cover for dry areas. It grows about four inches tall, spreads by creeping, and forms mats of tiny foliage. It is fine for between stepping stones and in rocky places. Propagate by dividing or making cuttings.

GROUND IVY, *Nepeta hederacea* (zones 3 to 9). A weed when found in lawns, this creeping perennial grows to three inches tall, forming a low mat that does well in both sun and shade. Propagate by dividing.

HONEYSUCKLE, *Lonicera japonica* (zones 5 to 9). This climbing, twisting, fragrant vine grows well in sun or partial shade and is excellent for getting fast growth on banks and other areas subject to erosion. It can become a pest, since it tends to cover and kill shrubs and even trees. It should be pruned each year: Be sure to clear away the cuttings, or they may take root. Propagate by dividing or making cuttings.

JAPANESE SPURGE, *Pachysandra terminalis* (zones 5 to 8). This evergreen grows six to twelve inches high and spreads by underground stems. It covers an area quickly and does well under trees and in other semishade. Propagate by dividing or making cuttings.

MEMORIAL ROSE, *Rose Wichuraiana* (zones 5 to 9). A low-growing, trailing plant with semi-evergreen foliage, memorial rose has fragrant two-inch, white flowers. It grows well on banks and sand dunes and is highly tolerant to salt spray. Propagate by planting seed or making cuttings.

PERIWINKLE, *Vinca minor* and *V. major* (zones 5 to 10). This popular evergreen, trailing plant has dark green foliage and small purple, blue, or white flowers. *V. minor* grows six inches tall and has small leaves; *V. major* grows eight inches tall and has larger leaves. Both grow well in full sun or partial shade. Propagate by dividing or making root cuttings.

ST. JOHN'S-WORT, *Hypericum calycinum* (zones 6 to 10). Also called Aaron's beard, this semi-evergreen shrub does well in semishade and sandy soil, growing nine to twelve inches tall. Its bright yellow flowers are seen from midsummer to frost, when the foliage turns red. Propagate by planting seed, dividing, or making cuttings.

SOUTH AFRICAN DAISY, *Gazania rigens* (zones 9 and 10). This orange-flowered plant grows six to nine inches tall, with light green foliage. It blooms throughout the spring and summer, and once established, will thrive with little water. Propagate by planting seed.

STRAWBERRY GERANIUM, *Saxifraga sarmentosa* (zones 7 to 9). This perennial grows to fifteen inches tall and spreads by runners. It is best in partial shade and is useful around the base of other plants, in rock gardens, and in areas of heavy clay. Propagate by making cuttings.

WANDERING JEW, *Zebrina pendula* (zone 10). Commonly found in greenhouses farther north, this perennial grows six to nine inches high, roots readily, and grows easily in the shade. Propagate by dividing or by making cuttings.

WEEPING LANTANA, *Lantana montevidensis* (zones 8 to 10). This trailing shrub has hairy branches up to three feet long. It grows best in sun and is highly salt tolerant. Propagate by cuttings or seed.

WINTER CREEPER, *Euonymus Fortunei* (zones 5 to 7). This evergreen ground cover, native to the eastern United States, does well in acid soils and moist, shady areas. It grows about four inches tall. Propagate by dividing.

SWEET WOODRUFF, *Galium odoratum*. Sweet woodruff is a spreading perennial, up to twelve inches in height. In early spring it bears delicate, bright green leaves, profusely scattered with tiny white starlike flowers. Freshly cut sprigs are often added to white wine to make traditional May wine. Sweet woodruff grows well in average soils, in both sun and shade, and spreads quickly and freely. Propagate by seeds or division.

Sweet woodruff.

Where can I find more information about ground covers to help me decide what would be good for my needs? I would especially like to see some examples.

As you drive around, look for the ground covers that do best in your area. You'll find them around houses, as well as in parks and other public places. Some of the best are along our highways, thanks to Mrs. Lyndon Johnson's promotion of programs for their development along federal highways. Sources of information include Extension Service specialists, garden centers, and state or city highway engineers.

I have purchased some junipers and cotoneasters to use as ground covers. How should I plant them?

The method of planting ground covers depends, of course, on the size of the plants selected. Large ones, such as junipers and cotoneasters, should be handled as described in the section on trees and shrubs (see pages 81–85).

What steps should I take to plant small ground covers?

- Mark places to dig planting holes, spacing them so the plants will cover the area when they reach maturity, and staggering every other row to avoid straight lines in any direction.
- Dig planting holes four to six inches wider and an inch or two deeper than the plant root ball. Place a mixture of peat moss and organic matter in the bottom of the hole.
- Set the plant in the hole, making certain it is set at the same height, in relation to ground level, that it was growing.
- Fill the hole with more peat moss-organic matter mixture, or with compost, packing it firmly around the plant, but leaving a slight indentation at the top to hold water.
- Water thoroughly.
- Pull any weeds that emerge.

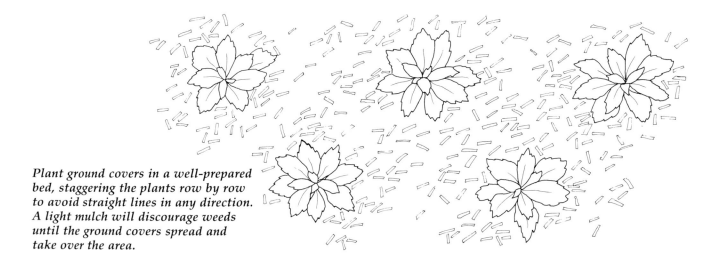

Plant ground covers in a well-prepared bed, staggering the plants row by row to avoid straight lines in any direction. A light mulch will discourage weeds until the ground covers spread and take over the area.

What can I do to beautify a large slope and manage erosion in my yard?

If your slope is steep, consider building a retaining wall (see pages 124–125). This may not only enhance your property visually, but it will also lessen the problem of erosion.

If you decide to use plantings, large plants such as creeping juniper, with roots that reach deep into the soil and spread in all directions, are best for steep slopes. Planting through sheets of plastic mulch will enable these plants to get established before being subjected to the threat of erosion.

In addition to erosion, moisture causes other problems on slopes. Because water flows off them so quickly, they often cannot build up the moisture reserve found in level areas. Thus, plants on them may be suffering from a lack of moisture when those in your garden have an ample supply. Remember to water plantings on slopes first.

Do ground covers require a lot of care?

Ground covers have the same needs for fertilizer and water as any other plants. Because of their spacing, however, young plants can be even more threatened by weeds than other new plants. Keep the weeds from taking over by light mulching, and pull up any weeds that break through the mulch as soon as possible. Avoid hoeing. Not only may you accidentally cut the roots of your plants but you may even promote the germination of more weed seeds.

Should I give my ground covers any winter protection?

In winter, evergreen plants, particularly, are often damaged by the sun. Waterproofing sprays, available at your garden center and applied in the fall, will greatly reduce the damage. The plants, too, can be protected with tree boughs or burlap laid over them.

How can I get my ground covers to move into new areas even more rapidly?

Once you have your ground cover established, you can enlarge it by propagation, either by cuttings or division.

Making tip cuttings is very easy. Get enough peat pots for the number of cuttings you want to make. Fill them with a potting mix of two parts sand and one part each of good soil and peat moss. Cut a three- to six-inch piece off the top of each plant. Strip the foliage from the lower section of each cutting where it will be below the soil line after planting. Treat each base with a root stimulant (available from a garden center). Insert each cutting into a peat pot; water thoroughly.

Place trays of these cuttings in the shade, cover them lightly with clear plastic, and continue to water regularly. Cuttings

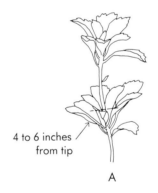

4 to 6 inches from tip

A

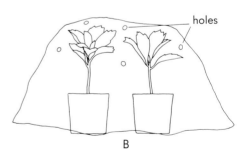

holes

B

(A) For tip cuttings, cut a 3- to 6-inch piece off the top of each plant; (B) treat cuttings with a root stimulant, place them in peat pots, cover them lightly with clear plastic, and keep them moist; when they begin to root, cut holes in the plastic to increase the air supply.

To propagate by division, dig out a clump of the plants including the roots, cut or pull them apart to form smaller plants, and replant them in enriched soil.

should begin to root in ten to thirty days. Pull one gently. If there is some resistance, it's a sign that the roots are forming. When this occurs, cut holes in the plastic to increase the air supply. Gradually increase the size of the holes so the cuttings will harden (become stronger). Finally, remove the cover. Ten days later, pinch back the tip of each cutting to promote branching.

If the tips are started in the spring, they can be transplanted to permanent sites in midsummer.

What does "propagation by division" mean?

Many plants, such as daylilies, can be propagated by division. To divide, dig up the mature plant, then cut or break off vigorous side shoots. Keep the clumps fairly large so they will provide cover the first year after being replanted. The best time to divide plants is in the late summer or fall in southern areas and in spring in northern areas.

What can be done with a narrow front lawn between an old-fashioned house with a high porch and the street, which is lined with large, old maples?

Instead of grass, which will not thrive in shade, especially under maples, try to establish a ground cover such as myrtle or pachysandra. Hide the porch foundation with a low hedge or an informal grouping of yews or Japanese holly.

I live in Southern California. How can I grow a dichondra lawn?

Dichondra is a creeping vine of the morning-glory family used for lawns in many desert areas where grasses will not grow well.

Daylilies are easily propagated by division.

Positive Images, Jerry Howard

Buy flats of the plants, and plant them about a foot apart. If well watered, they will spread rapidly. Such a lawn requires mowing three or four times a year, frequent feeding with a balanced commercial fertilizer, and plenty of water if it is to remain green and dense.

I have seen a ground cover used on highway banks. It has white and pink flowers in the late spring and seems to cover the bank with a thick coat. What is it?

My guess is that what you're seeing is crown vetch, *Coronilla varia*, which is a favorite of highway crews because it halts erosion, requires no maintenance, and will grow in most soils and climates in the United States. Don't think of this solely as a plant for highway banks. It's useful for home landscapes to cover problem areas. You can buy crowns of this plant or plant seed.

4 *Flower Gardens in the Landscape*

I f you think of shrubs and trees as the frame for your landscaping, you can then make it come alive with the many colors, sizes, and shapes of bright perennials. Perennials are plants that have a life cycle of three or more seasons, in contrast to annuals and biennials, whose life cycles are one and two years, respectively. In the careful structuring of your yard or garden, perennials are the jewels to be shown off and admired. As they flourish and demand to be thinned or divided, they make splendid gifts. Gardeners who may not know the botanical names of their perennials can—and will—recite in detail the circumstances of receiving them. From alyssum and aster to yarrow and yucca, their values are many:

- If you find you've planted one in a poor location, it's only a few minutes' work to move it, and most move without damage to the plant.
- They are among the less expensive offerings at your garden center. They are also often easy to propagate yourself: many can be grown from seed, and single plants can often be multiplied by division or other forms of propagation (see pages 89–90).
- Many are disease-resistant and easy to maintain, requiring no more than good soil, sunshine, and moisture.
- Perhaps their greatest asset, after their beauty and hardiness, is their versatility. Need a row of plants to line a walk? Something to fill that shaded spot in the corner of a lot? A bright addition to a clump of drab shrubs? A bed of cutting

◀ *Low-growing moss pink, or moss phlox, brings splendid color to a sunny slope.*

93

Landscaping comes alive with the many colors, shapes, and sizes of bright annuals and perennials.

flowers? Look at the perennials for any such needs. (A bed of perennials along a fence, walk, or patio is often called a flower *border*.)

I had always imagined that creating a perennial garden took quite a lot of special knowledge and care. Isn't that true?

Perennials *can* be challenging, and even the best gardeners admit they still have much to learn about such things as the lighting preferences of their many daylilies. Each perennial has its particular fascination, however, and your own favorites, some of which are quite easy to grow, will soon give you confidence.

What perennials are good for beginning gardeners?

Many of the ground covers and shrubs discussed in other sections of this book are true perennials—particularly those that flower, such as barrenwort, bugleweed, creeping lily turf, thyme, crown vetch, bergenia, sandwort, and gazania. In addition, our perennial list gives a small sampling of some all-time favorite perennial flowers. All fare well in zones 4 to 8.

I have read that a garden should not compete with a view. Why?

The intimate detail of a garden suffers by comparison with a wide view into the surrounding landscape. It is usually wiser to enclose the garden, shutting out the wide view and leaving an opening framed by trees or evergreen shrubs, so the view becomes a focal point seen from the house or patio.

Is there a rule for good proportion in the size of a garden?

No, but there are guidelines. Oblong areas are more pleasing when they are about one and a half times as long as they are wide. An oblong is better than a square, and an oval is more effective than a circle.

What's the difference between a formal and a naturalistic garden?

Formal designs use straight lines and circular curves or arcs. A formal garden thus is a composition in geometric lines—squares, oblongs, circles, or parts of these. It need not be large, nor must it be filled with architectural embellishment. Formality emphasizes lines; informality emphasizes space and uses long, free-flowing curves.

In landscaping, what is a focal point?

It's the point of highest interest in the development of the design. For example, it might be a garden fountain or a group of particularly striking plants. Planners often start with a focal point, then build the rest of the design around it.

SELECTED PERENNIALS

ASTER, *Aster*. Most of the many varieties grow one to four feet tall and blossom with a wide range of colors, particularly lavender and purple, in late summer and fall. The spectacular blossoms of new hybrids are available in even more colors. Propagate asters by dividing.

BEE BALM, *Monarda didyma*. Bee balm grows three or more feet tall with scarlet blossoms in the summer that attract bees and hummingbirds. It is easy to cover an area with these flowers, since they spread rapidly. Propagate by division.

CANTERBURY BELLS, *Campanula Medium*. Two to four feet high, with violet flowers throughout summer, Canterbury Bells are actually biennial. Many species of *Campanula*, however, from small rock garden plants to much larger ones, are perennials. Start *Campanula* from seed. Perennial varieties may be divided.

CHINESE LANTERNS, *Physalis alkekengi*. Chinese lanterns grow two feet high, with white flowers that become small red berries enclosed in large orange "lanterns," popular for dried flower arrangements. Propagate this plant by seed or division.

Positive Images, Gary Mottau

Canterbury bells.

DAYLILY, *Hemerocallis*. There are hundreds of hybrid daylilies, some growing up to five feet tall, but most two to three feet. New varieties appear yearly. They thrive in sunshine as well as in partial shade, and offer a long-lasting display of blossoms of many hues. These are an excellent choice for specimen plants, for both the beginner and the specialist. Propagate daylilies by division.

MONKSHOOD, *Aconitum Napellus*. Monkshood grows three to four feet tall, with blue to purple flowers in summer. It thrives as a sunny border. Some varieties are shorter and are available in a variety of colors. Propagate monkshood by division.

Positive Images, Jerry Howard

Phlox.

PEONY, *Paeonia*. The many species and hybrids of peonies offer diversity in your garden. Most are three to five feet tall, with either simple, single flowers or mammoth showy blooms in spring, ranging from white, pink, and yellow to red. Propagate peonies by dividing the root clump.

PHLOX, *Phlox paniculata*. Phlox grows about four feet tall, with spreading clusters of vividly colored flowers. It likes full sun and rich soil, and is good for borders. Propagate by dividing roots.

TICKSEED, *Coreopsis*. Some 100 species, most of them one to three feet in height, have large yellow (some white and pink) blossoms throughout summer. Propagate by dividing, or from seed.

YARROW, *Achillea filipendulina*. Yarrow may reach up to four feet, with yellow flowers in summer. It should be grown in sun, and makes a good border. Propagate by division.

How do you determine the size of a garden?

The best rule is to decide how well you enjoy garden work, and then plan as much as you can care for easily. You should keep the design of the entire lot in mind, but the details can be simple. Instead of lawns, you might design areas of ground cover (low-growing plants that cover the ground instead of lawn grass) interspersed with sections of gravel and paving for patios and walks. Accent with shrubs that stay in scale as they mature. Make flower beds only as large as you can manage to keep tended.

Should a garden have a lawn space in the middle?

Not all gardens should be designed this way, but there are many advantages to this type of layout. A grass panel serves as a foreground to the floral displays, as well as a space for chairs and tables. In addition, a continuous border garden is easier to maintain than one made up of many individual beds.

Must a garden be level?

Definitely not. A sloping garden, perhaps with a retaining wall, a walk, or even a small stream, offers many more possibilities than a flat area. A naturalistic garden should have a natural grade, rather than being level or smoothly sloping.

What sort of a garden would you plant on a plot thirty by sixty feet?

If this is a flat area, it can be effectively developed by creating an open grass or gravel panel down the center, with flower

Positive Images, Jerry Howard

A slope provides an ideal setting for, and is itself enhanced by, a naturalistic garden.

A flower bed full of old-fashioned varieties serves well as the foundation planting against an old colonial house.

borders along the sides backed by shrub borders or hedges, all leading to a strong focal point, such as a lily pool or patio.

Which is better for a small place, a formal or an informal garden?

Topography, more than size, controls the design. On flat ground near buildings, a rectangular, formal type of design is easier to adapt. On rough land—particularly on slopes and in wooded areas—greater informality is desirable.

Can I plant flowers along the foundation of our house?

Of course you can, but in most cases, shrubs and ground covers with flowers planted in front of them give a better effect than flowers alone, which are apt to look too small and inadequate near a house foundation.

What perennials will grow in a sunny, dry area? I prefer showy flowers.

Try the bright gold gloriosa daisy with its prominent dark brown center, the gay orange Oriental poppy, the red, gold, and yellow, daisylike blanketflower, and the many colorful varieties of daylilies. Many of the perennial asters will do well in sunny, dry spots as well.

How can I make my flower border more interesting?

Plantings made up of only one kind of plant, or even a few similar varieties, are monotonous and uninteresting. Use occasional plants of different varieties, sizes, and colors to provide accents. For example, clumps of tall blue delphinium blossoms add drama to a border of daisies and bee balm.

What plants (tall, medium, and low) may I use in a garden shaded by oak trees? What soil improvements should be made to overcome acidity from oaks?

You won't need to improve the soil if you select native wildflowers, such as cypripedium, fern, mayapple, and jack-in-the-pulpit. For taller plants, you have a wide choice in such shrubs as holly, mountain laurel, azalea, blueberry, and rhododendron. A combination of these would be especially attractive.

What would grow well along the north-facing wall of our house, which gets little sun?

Many perennials and wildflowers do well in such settings, including columbine, lady's slipper, hepatica, epimedium, bleeding heart, foxglove, fern rue, Virginia bluebells, anemone, primrose, blue langwort, monkshood, shooting star, rue, and some daylilies.

Which flowering plants will grow in an area that receives only two or three hours of strong sun daily?

Daylily, bleeding heart with its intriguing and distinctive, dropping blossoms, primrose in a variety of colors from pinks and blues to yellows and white, and hosta with its tall, nodding blue, violet, or white spiky blooms.

Positive Images, Jerry Howard

Bleeding heart thrives in partial shade.

What plants will grow in dense shade around the base of a large tree? Must I put them in pots because of the tree roots?

Few plants will subsist on what's left in the soil after the roots of a large tree have filled the surface and used all available food. Try digging out pockets in the ground, filling them with good loam, and planting one of the following: violets, creeping mahonia, periwinkle, English ivy, or pachysandra. If these fail, you would be better off to spread bark mulch over the area and leave it bare of plants. Potted plants, although of only temporary value, can add welcome spots of color in such a setting; use such shade plants as impatiens and begonia.

Would a garden plot laid out on the edge of a lake be satisfactory?

Why not? Have the soil tested by your Extension Service or do it yourself with a soil-testing kit, since the humus content at such a location may be low. The only special consideration you may need to be aware of is that the presence of the lake may influence frost conditions at your garden site. If it is near a large lake, the water may give off heat during the fall and protect your area from early frosts. If you are near a small body of water in a valley, you may experience exactly the opposite effect, since the cold air of early frosts tends to pour down hills and make your area colder than those higher on the hills.

Is garden lighting costly to maintain?

No. The lights are turned on for such a short time that the cost of electricity is negligible. Initially, the installation of weatherproof lights, wiring, and sockets might seem expensive, but by illuminating parts of the garden and its paths at night you gain new opportunities to appreciate the garden. Solar-powered garden lights are also readily available and not terribly expensive.

Positive Images, Gary Mottau

A variety of heights, colors, and textures make this garden stunningly successful.

When you plant bulbs, you plant a hope in tomorrow. Triggered into motion by time or temperature, bulbs are one of the most reliable of plants, welcoming spring when most needed, long before color is contributed to the garden by any other plant.

Spring bulbs are winter hardy: they are planted in fall, grow and bloom in spring, and then lie dormant for a year. They do not need to be dug out of the ground except when they are divided. Both true bulbs (daffodils, hyacinths, glory of the snow, and others) and corms (crocus) are classified as bulbs because of their unique food-storing capabilities and their growth habits. Both are planted while dormant and then grow, bloom, and store food before going dormant again.

True bulbs are actually complete plants within a tiny package. Slice into a bulb and you will see the future roots, stems, leaves,

SPRING BULBS

Maggie Oster

Daffodils are an excellent bulb to naturalize, but they must be left undisturbed until their foliage dies back.

and flowers. Fleshy scales surrounding this future growth contain all the necessary food for the bulb to grow. After the bulb has bloomed, food for the next season is manufactured in the leaves and transferred to the underground portion to start the chain again the following year.

Corms are modified stems filled with food storage tissue. They are usually short and squat and covered with a meshlike material. After a corm blooms, the original corm disappears and a new one forms for next year's growth.

When should bulbs be planted?

You can plant spring-flowering bulbs any time in fall until the soil freezes; if you can't plant them all at once, start with the smaller, earlier flowering bulbs such as crocus, squill, glory-of-the-snow, winter aconite, and other tiny bulbs, and then plant tulips and daffodils.

Where can I plant bulbs?

When you plant spring bulbs, set early charmers where you and passers-by will notice them the most. Besides growing *in* the lawn, they will do well around the base of trees near the house, or in small clumps near the front door. Line the path to the door. Squeeze them into the corner of the rock garden or use them as a border in front of foundation plantings.

Our yard is rather shady. Does this mean I can't grow bulbs?

Many bulbs like full sun, but since most spring bulbs bloom before the trees leaf out, shade from trees is usually not troublesome. However, if many hours of shade are cast from the side of the house, that will be a problem and you should look for another place to plant. You will find that those bulbs planted in a shaded spot will bloom a little later, will have a more intense color, and will last somewhat longer.

How should I prepare the soil for bulbs?

Good soil preparation is critical to a successful bulb garden, as it is to other gardens. Because bulb roots reach deep, you'll need to spade and prepare the bed to a depth of twelve inches. Look for soil with good drainage so that bulbs and roots won't rot. Provide good aeration as well as nutrients by adding organic matter, such as peat moss, compost, or leaf mold, equal to twenty-five percent of the soil volume. To encourage root growth, add phosphorus-rich bonemeal to the bottom of each planting hole as well.

How do I actually go about setting the bulbs in the ground?

You can prepare holes by one of two methods: you can either dig individual holes for each bulb, or you can dig out an entire area, put the bulbs in place and restore the soil. The latter is the better idea if you are planting a large number of bulbs.

How deep should bulbs be planted?

Consult the chart on pages 102-103 for advice, or plant a bulb to a depth approximately three times its width.

Do bulb plantings need mulching?

It's an especially good idea to mulch bulbs, as mulch can help to keep the smaller bulbs from heaving out of the ground during the winter. Use an organic mulch such as leaf mold, compost, bean hulls, wood chips, or pine needles to enrich the soil as the mulch breaks down.

Do established bulbs need to be fertilized?

Even though you properly prepared your bulb bed at planting time, you will need to add extra fertilizer each year to keep the bulbs healthy and flowering at their peak. When bulb foliage begins to emerge in spring, sprinkle fertilizer on the ground and water it in. For maximum results, feed again as the foliage starts to yellow. Use an all-purpose fertilizer such as 5-10-5 (see pages 30–34) or a specially prepared bulb food.

Do bulbs need extra water?

Once bulbs start to poke their way through the ground in spring, they will need a lot of moisture, so water deeply if the spring is a dry one. Proper flowering and growth depend on sufficient water reaching deep into the root zone.

I've seen many tulips planted so that they stand like soldiers in a row. How can I avoid this unappealing arrangement?

Almost without exception, bulbs look better when planted in clumps of at least three. The smaller the bulb, the more flowers you need in the clump. For example, plant four clumps with three tulips in each clump across a nine-foot section of the foundation planting, rather than planting the tulips single file, nine inches apart in an empty-looking line.

Bulbs can also be naturalized into an informal look, particularly appropriate in woodland settings. Left to multiply on their own, their colony will increase. Select a spot for your naturalistic planting that will not have to be disturbed until after the flowers and foliage have faded away.

When planting, toss bulbs randomly onto the planting bed, and then plant them where they fall. Even if you have to adjust them slightly to maintain correct spacing, you will still be able to achieve a less contrived effect than if you had tried to arrange them.

SELECTED SPRING BULBS

ANEMONE, GRECIAN WINDFLOWER, *Anemone blanda*. Anemones are small and daisylike with two- to three-inch flowers in shades of blue, pink, or white with bright yellow centers. They bloom in early to mid-spring. Foliage is starburstlike and grows close to the ground. Plant two inches deep, four to six inches apart, in well-drained soil in full sun or light shade.

CAMASSIA, *Camassia*. One of the last blooming of the spring bulbs, camassia have loose spikes of pale blue, star-shaped flowers on three-inch stems over large clumps of strap-shaped foliage. Plant four inches deep, four to six inches apart, in moist soil in part sun.

CROCUS, *Crocus*. Although not the first bulbs to bloom, crocus are regarded by many as the first sign of spring. Hybrid crocus bear white, purple, lavender, or yellow blossoms. Long, narrow foliage is deep green, often with a stripe. These are very hardy bulbs. Plant three to four inches deep, three inches apart, in rich, well-drained soil in full or part sun.

CROWN IMPERIAL, *Fritillaria imperialis*. On top of a thirty- to forty-eight-inch stem, yellow, red, or orange flowers hang in a tuft under a crown of foliage. Leaves clothe the stalk up to the flower. Fragrance can be very heavy. Plant five inches deep, eighteen inches apart, in average soil in part sun.

DAFFODILS AND JONQUILS, *Narcissus*. A welcome sight of midspring, daffodils and jonquils bloom atop six- to twelve-inch stems in a variety of flower shapes, including trumpets, doubles, and large and small cups. Some have a number of tiny blooms along the stem. The flowers are white, yellow, or a combination of both, or pale pink. Many are fragrant. Perfect for naturalizing, but their foliage hangs on until early summer; be sure to plant them where they can be left undisturbed. Plant six inches deep, six to twelve inches apart, in well-drained, rich soil in full sun or part shade.

DOGTOOTH VIOLET, TROUT LILY, *Erythronium*. For a wildflower look in the garden, the dogtooth violet's bloom is lilylike and white, rose, violet, or yellow, nodding on a six- to twelve-inch stem. Two strap-shaped leaves are often mottled. Its names come from the facts that the corm resembles a tooth, the leaves are mottled like a trout's back, and the flower blooms at trout season. Plant three inches deep, four inches apart, in moist, rich soil in shade.

GLORY OF THE SNOW, *Chionodoxa luciliae*. One of the earliest to bloom, glory of the snow's six-petalled, starlike flowers are mostly blue with a light center, although there are white and pink forms.

Spikes of blooms are four to five inches high from the center of straplike leaves. Easy to grow, it never needs dividing. Leave undisturbed after blooming to form colonies. Extremely hardy. Plant four inches deep, three inches apart, in dry soil in full sun or part shade.

GRAPE HYACINTH, *Muscari*. Cone-shaped clusters of drooping flowers are bright blue to purple in mid-spring. Foliage appears again in fall and can be untidy looking. Plant three inches deep, four inches apart, in average soil in full to part sun.

GUINEA HEN FLOWER, *Fritillaria meleagris*. Six-petalled, two-inch, purple and white checkered flowers resembling a lampshade or an upside-down tulip appear in mid-spring on stems six to twelve inches high. Leaves are thin and grasslike. Plant four inches deep, five inches apart, in average soil in full sun to part shade.

HYACINTH, *Hyacinthus hybrids*. The tall, rounded, fragrant clusters of small, star-shaped flowers bloom in shades of red, white, pink, blue, purple, or yellow. The six- to eight-inch blooms grow from the center of straplike leaves. They will lose some of their compactness after several years and will need to be replaced. Plant six inches deep, six inches apart, in rich, well-drained soil in full to part sun.

IRIS, *Iris*. There are two irises grown from bulbs; the others, grown from rhizomes, are categorized as perennials. Reticulatas bloom in early spring and grow four to eight inches high. Foliage is grassy. Dutch iris, orchidlike and a good cut flower, bloom in late spring with stems up to twenty-four inches high. Flowers of both are purple, blue, yellow, or white. Plant four inches deep, three to four inches apart, in well-drained soil in full sun.

PUSCHKINIA, *Puschkinia*. Small, star-shaped flowers of white or pale blue with a blue stripe are among the first bulbs to bloom. Do not disturb them, and they will quickly colonize. Plant three inches deep, three inches apart, in average soil in full to part sun.

SIBERIAN SQUILL, *scilla sibirica*. Early blooming, the deep blue to purple flowers grow four to six inches high and are surrounded by broad leaves. Bloom spikes are made up of individual pendant flowers. Do not disturb after planting. Plant two to three inches deep, three inches apart, in average soil in full to part sun.

SNOWDROPS, *Galanthus nivalis*. Another gem among early blooming bulbs, snowdrops can appear while snow is still on the ground. Perfect for a woodland setting, three-part flowers drop from a thin stem about four to six inches tall. Blooms are

Anemones, grape hyacinths, daffodils, and tulips welcome spring with a dependability and ease of mainte-nance that all gardeners appreciate.

white with waxy green tips on the inside that are seen as the petals open in the sun. Four- to six-inch high foliage is greenish gray and grasslike. Plant four inches deep, two inches apart, in average soil in full sun or part shade.

STAR OF BETHLEHEM, *Ornithogalum umbellatum.* Star of Bethlehem, named for the six-petalled, star-shaped flowers that bloom in clusters on stems six inches high, will thrive under the poorest conditions. Each white flower is about one inch wide, with a thin green stripe on the outside of each petal, a black center, and yellow stamens. Foliage is very dense and grassy. A good cut flower. Plant four inches deep, three to four inches apart, in average to poor soil in full to part sun.

SUMMER SNOWFLAKE, *Leucojum aestivum.* The summer snowflake blooms in mid-spring, but is so named to distinguish it from the earlier blooming spring snowflake. It has a cluster of five or six white bell-shaped flowers hanging from atop a nine- to twelve-inch stem, and resembles a large lily-of-the-valley. Plant four inches deep, four inches apart, in average soil in part shade.

TULIP, *Tulipa.* For a tall, stately, formal look, tulips are the spring favorite for massed beds of red, white, blue, purple, yellow, pink, coral, or even black color. Flowers range from classic cottage or Darwin tulips, to fringed parrot, pointed lily, and starburst miniatures. Many of the hybrids grow to thirty inches. Plant six inches deep, four to six inches apart, in rich, fast-draining soil in full sun.

WINTER ACONITE, *Eranthis hyemalis.* This early-to-bloom plant often appears when there is still snow on the ground. Six-petalled, waxy, sunny yellow, sweetly scented blooms are about two inches across and resemble buttercups. The shiny, thick, deep green foliage rays out from underneath the flower in a starlike pattern. The tuber must not be allowed to dry out, so plant it right away. Plant two inches deep, three to four inches apart, in rich, moist soil in full or part sun.

WOOD HYACINTH, *Scilla hispanica.* Loose clusters of pink or blue, bell-shaped flowers resemble informal hyacinths. Blooming in late spring, it grows to eighteen inches. Plant three inches deep, six inches apart, in average, moist soil in part shade.

Is there anything I should do after the bulbs have bloomed?

When tulips, daffodils, hyacinths, and other large bulbs have finished blooming, cut off the flowers (called ''deadheading'') to prevent seed formation and to direct energy to the bulb. Smaller bulbs can be left to go to seed, which will scatter and increase the colony.

Never remove the leaves until they have completely browned and pull away from the plant easily. As the foliage matures it is manufacturing the food for next year's growth. If you remove the leaves too soon, the bulb will not bloom the following spring. Where bulbs are planted in the lawn, do not mow the grass until the foliage has browned.

To achieve a neater look, you can braid the foliage of larger bulbs or twirl it into a circle until the foliage ripens.

Spring bulbs are beautiful while they are blooming, but what about the empty spaces after they have died away?

If you interplant bulbs with a ground cover, you will not have to worry. In flower beds, add annuals as soon as they can be planted in the spring; no harm is done to bulb plantings to overplant them this way. Perennials also make excellent companions to bulbs, for they come into bloom about the time the bulbs fade. If possible, divide and replant both the bulbs and the perennials in the spring when you can see the location of both to avoid accidental injury to bulbs and roots.

Will I have to dig up my bulbs once they are planted?

Many small bulbs, such as quill, can be forgotten once planted. Daffodils and crocus, on the other hand, need to be dug and divided every five or six years when the clumps get too large, and bloom size and number begin to decline. Tulips and hyacinths do not multiply in the climate found in most parts of this continent, and so diminish in size and need to be replaced every several years.

The best time to divide and replant bulbs is in spring right after the foliage starts to yellow: It's easier to locate and avoid damaging or cutting the bulbs when you can still see the leaves. Also, when you replant bulbs in the spring, you'll know where gaps are in the garden and you won't plant them on top of each other.

When moving bulbs, dig them carefully so as not to disturb the roots and replant them immediately using the same techniques as you do when planting new bulbs in the fall. Leave the foliage in place after planting and let it mature as though the bulb had not been moved.

Do bulbs have many disease and insect problems?

If a bulb shows sign of disease in the form of a misshapen or discolored flower, it's best to dig it out and prevent the problem from spreading. Few insects bother bulbs.

Whatever you are planting—lawns, trees, shrubs, flowers, or vegetables—you must know the soil on your property. You will soon discover one area is just fine and another is quite poor, perhaps because dirt was dumped there while excavating for the house foundation. Further, you must understand what you can do about these conditions.

The first possibility is to select plants that will survive in the available soil. There are plants that will thrive even in conditions as bad as the nearly pure sand of seaside gardens. A better approach is, first, to change the texture and fertility of your soil by adding organic material to the soil in large quantities (see page 7). This material is attacked by the billions of microorganisms in the soil in order to break it down into a form that the plants can use. Second, you should test the pH, or acidity, of your soil to determine whether it is in the 6.0 to 7.0 range that is best for growing most plants. This can be done by sending soil samples to your Extension Service or by obtaining a soil-testing kit at your garden center. Whether you are growing flowers or vegetables, constant soil improvement is essential, and there are many ways to do this.

YOUR GARDEN SOIL

A successful perennial garden is dependent upon thorough soil preparation before planting.

I've heard of soil nutrients. What are they, and why are they important to plants?

The "big three" in nutrient elements for plants are nitrogen, phosphorus, and potassium, listed in that order on bags of fertilizer. Thus, a bag marked 5-10-5 has 5 per cent nitrogen, 10 percent phosphorus, and 5 percent potassium. One criticism often made of chemical fertilizers is that they burn foliage. While it is true that these fertilizer salts can suck water out of leaves and roots, you can avoid this by carefully using recommended rates and watering them in as soon as you apply them.

Organic fertilizers have the same elements as chemical fertilizers, but often in a highly complex form. They are thus unavailable to plants until they have been digested or broken down into simpler forms by soil organisms. Because these organisms are partially dormant at temperatures below 60° F., they are not effective in early spring for hardy crops. On the plus side, in addition to their nutrient value, organic fertilizers add a great deal of organic matter to the soil, which pure chemical or mineral fertilizers do not.

All of the elements in fertilizers play roles in the growing of plants.

Nitrogen is vital to the formation of all proteins. It is an essential element of chlorophyll, the green chemical that permits plants to manufacture starches and sugars. Many of the compounds in plants, such as amino acids, and aromatic compounds, must have nitrogen. It is the "grow" element, and overuse of it results in soft, lush growth. Stunted growth and pale yellow foliage, on the other hand, are signs of a nitrogen deficiency.

In place of commercial fertilizers, organic gardeners often use cottonseed meal (about 3-to-5-2-1), blood meal (12.5-1.3-.7), or fish meal (10.5-6-0). The latter is also a good source of phosphorus. (See also pages 44-46.)

Phosphorus is needed for good root and stem development. The usual commercial source is superphosphate; organic gardeners turn to bone meal, phosphate rock, or soft phosphate. Signs of a phosphorus deficiency are stunted growth and purple coloring of leaves and stems.

In Victorian days, bone meal was one of the few good fertilizers available. Thus, many gardeners had bone grinders in their potting sheds to grind up fresh, raw bone with scraps of meat still clinging to it. It was a rich addition to the soil.

Potassium, in the form of potash, is abundant in most American soils, but may be soilbound and thus not available to plants. For healthy plants, it may be essential to add potassium to the soil. Bronzing of leaves, slow growth, and unusually high incidence of disease are all signs of a deficiency of this element. Sulphate of potash and muriate of potash are available as commercial products. Organic gardeners turn to kelp meal, wood ashes, crushed granite, and greensand.

If wood ashes are used, they should be applied before planting and thoroughly mixed with the soil. The reason for this is that until the potassium they contain has been dissolved and absorbed by the soil, a free lye solution is present that can damage roots for two to three days after application. Ashes, too, act to sweeten (raise the pH of) the soil, and overuse of them, by spreading ashes from a woodstove or fireplace in the same area year after year, can result in a soil that has too high a pH.

How can I improve the nutrient content of my soil?

One of the easiest ways is to make compost. This process is often made to sound so scientific that beginners avoid trying it, but it can be done very easily.

A simple compost bin made from a cylinder of sturdy wire mesh.

Start by enclosing an area about four by four feet with chicken wire or boards spaced to permit air to circulate. Then pile up the organic refuse from your home, lawn, and gardens—vegetable scraps, grass clippings and leaves, garden refuse. Occasionally toss on a shovelful or two of soil, and keep the pile moist—not drenched, just moist.

The compost process will be speeded if you turn the pile over once or twice during the season, forking it from one enclosure to another. But this isn't necessary if you can wait a year to use the compost.

Some materials compost much faster than others. Leaves and hay compost very slowly. The process is speeded if the leaves are ground up. Grass cuttings are just the opposite. They get so hot in a matter of hours that their value is lost. So, instead of dumping baskets of grass clippings on the top of the pile, mix them with leaves or hay.

Don't compost piles attract dogs?

Avoid adding meat scraps and bones to the pile, and you shouldn't have a problem.

I worry that compost piles might give off offensive odors. Is this so?

It is very unlikely. If you smell anything at all, the odor will remind you of the woods. If there *is* an objectionable smell, add dried leaves, hay, or straw to the pile and work it in. Too much moisture is occasionally responsible for unpleasant aromas.

Aren't compost piles eyesores?

Compost piles have a reputation for being unsightly, and therefore are tucked back in the far reaches of a lot. Often this means the pile is far from both the source of materials that go into it and the place where it will be spread. Better to have it near both, where experienced gardeners will see and admire it. If you wish, plant a shrub or two to hide it from the eyes of those less knowledgeable in the ways of gardening.

What is the quickest way to bring an old, used garden spot back into quick production?

Spade in organic matter in the fall or plant a green manure (see page 44) crop. In the spring, apply superphosphate, hoe, rake, and plant. Add a complete fertilizer just before planting and again during the summer.

My flowers grow very poorly and usually die before their time. What causes this?

The chances are that your soil lacks fertility, moisture-holding capacity, and aeration. Additions of fertilizers and compost should correct these conditions.

My annuals and perennials grow tall and spindly. Could this be due to overfertilization, lack of sun, or lack of some fertilizer element? The garden site receives sunlight half the day.

The spindly growth may be due to lack of sunlight, poor drainage or compacted soil, improper fertilization, or any combination of these. If you have been gardening in the same area

For convenience keep your compost pile near the garden.

Walter Chandoha

for several years, it is quite probable that the amount of sunlight the plants receive has decreased, due to growth of nearby trees. Try to alter this. Improve the drainage and aeration of the soil (see pages 4-8), and choose a fertilizer with high proportions of phosphorus and potassium in relation to nitrogen, perhaps for a few years (see pages 30-31).

I have been raising flowers on the same ground for some time. What can I use to keep it in shape?

Incorporate organic matter, such as leaves or peat moss, in the soil between the plants during the spring or summer. Apply a good complete fertilizer, such as 5-10-5, in the spring.

Is it advisable to apply lime and commercial fertilizer on the snow during the winter for absorption when the snow melts?

For some flowers (and vegetables), lime and commercial fertilizers can be applied in the fall or winter, but in most cases it is more efficient to apply them in the spring. Chemical fertilizers, particularly, will leach out and be lost over a winter.

I hear people talking about the sandy soil or the clay soil on their property. How do they know which is which?

Most of them probably guess—and some of them guess wrong. If you want to be sure, follow the suggestions on page 6 to determine what type soil you have. Different soil types require different approaches to gardening and soil treatment, whether you are growing lawns, trees and shrubs, or flowers and vegetables.

How can I use my compost?

Compost can be used in many ways, especially to be dug into the soil to improve both its texture and fertility. If you have a lot of compost, screen it and use it as a lawn topdressing, or spread it around flowers, shrubs, and vegetables to stimulate their growth.

What can I put into my compost pile?

This page isn't large enough to give you a complete answer. In general, add about anything that is organic, except for meat scraps (which encourage animal pests). From your garden and house, heap on weeds, grass clippings, leaves, table scraps, wood shavings and sawdust (though these are slow to compost), and even the contents of the vacuum cleaner. If you have them, add animal manures, peat moss, ground corn cobs, and commercial fertilizer. The fall is an excellent time to get a compost pile going, since there is a lot of material available from lawns and gardens.

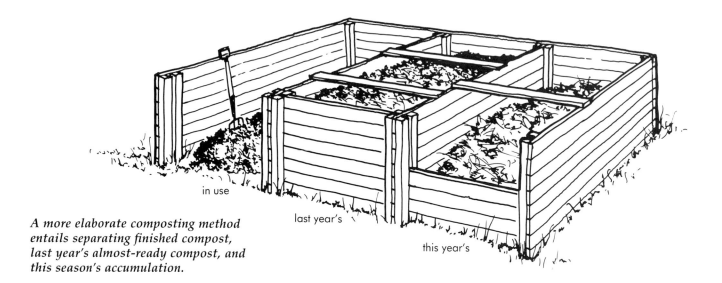

in use

last year's

this year's

A more elaborate composting method entails separating finished compost, last year's almost-ready compost, and this season's accumulation.

I was poking a stick into my compost pile to permit air to get into it, and touched the end of the stick when I pulled it out. To my surprise, it was more than warm—it was hot. I put a thermometer into the pile, and it rose to nearly 150°F. Should the pile be that hot?

That's a good sign that you've created a pile with an excellent blend of materials, and you'll have compost to use in a few weeks. To further encourage the process, wait until the pile cools a bit, then turn it over, working the outer layer into the center. This time the pile probably will not become as hot.

Are wood ashes better than coal ashes for a garden?

Wood ashes and coal ashes serve two distinct purposes. The former adds potassium to the soil, the latter improves the soil texture.

The soil in my front yard is extremely sandy. What flowers can I plant there?

You should first try to improve the soil by adding topsoil plus organic matter, such as peat moss, manure, or compost, and then working in fertilizer. If after trying these improvements, you find the soil is still quite sandy, fertilize the plants several times during the growing season, since many of the nutrients you apply will readily wash away. Flowers you might select for such soil include portulaca, California poppy, annual phlox, calliopsis, cockscomb, morning glory, anthemis, aster, baby's-breath, liatris, or yucca.

Can coal ashes be used to loosen clay soil?

Only if they have been exposed to weather to leach out harmful substances, such as toxic quantities of sulfur. You should also break up any pieces more than a quarter-inch in diameter. Prepared this way, a two-inch layer can be tilled into the clay.

My flower bed is heavy clay soil that is difficult to work up. Would well-rotted manure and wood ashes be a benefit?

Yes. You could add as much as ten pounds of ashes per 100 square feet, plus a six-inch layer of the manure. Fine cinders, too, would be beneficial. Till all of this well into the clay.

My ground gets hard and dry on the surface, so that it is difficult for young shoots to break through. It is soft enough beneath the surface. What can I do?

Incorporate well-rotted compost, peat moss, or a one-half-inch thick layer of vermiculite into the upper surface to prevent crusting.

What soil is best for a mixed flower border?

A slightly acid (pH 6.5), sandy loam, with manure, compost, and/or peat moss worked in. It's difficult to overdo the organic material when preparing a perennial garden, as once you plant you won't be able to get in easily to work soil amendments down around the plant roots.

Are earthworms harmful or beneficial in the garden? I find that they eat all the humus in the soil.

Earthworms are a nuisance in the green house or in potted plants, and they tend to leave unsightly piles of dirt on lawns. But in gardens, their constant working through the soil—eating, digesting, and eliminating waste—aerates the soil, a far greater benefit than any possible trouble they cause. Furthermore, their very presence is a sign of good soil, filled with the nutrients on which they—and your plants—thrive.

What is vermiculite?

It is a form of mica, heated so that it explodes, much like popcorn. It is sterile, holds moisture, and if not overwatered, allows air to reach the roots of plants. It is excellent for rooting cuttings and starting seeds. Use a planting flat with a window-screen wire bottom, for if overwatered, it will get soggy.

I've heard of "Cornell mix." What is it and when is it used?

This is an old favorite artificial soil mix used by gardeners for many years to start seedlings. To make a peck of the mix, combine the following:

    4 quarts vermiculite
    4 quarts shredded peat moss
    1 teaspoon 20-percent superphosphate
    1 tablespoon ground dolomitic limestone

5 Structures in the Landscape

N ow that your healthy green lawn is well underway and many of your trees, shrubs, and flowers are in place, you may wish to turn to ways of making movement around your yard pleasant and of defining your property or parts of it: paths, patios, and walls or fences. Your prime criterion should be to make these structures enhance but not intrude on your plantings. They should look as though they belong there naturally, even though you have constructed them.

A concrete walk may be the best answer for the entrance to your house, but for other areas, alternative materials are preferable. Your choice depends largely on the style of your house, the size and style of the area around the house, and the expected traffic on the path. Garden paths can be made of grass, wood chips and bark, wood sections, gravel, flagstone and slate, or bricks.

WALKS AND PATHS

What materials do you suggest for paths, and how do you determine which materials are best in specific situations?

A *grass* walk between flower beds is attractive and a good choice if the traffic will not be too heavy. Such a walk requires no extra care other than feeding the grass often enough to encourage its growth. For better wear, yet still a natural-looking path, set twelve-inch *stepping stones* into the lawn about twelve inches apart (a comfortable stride). Cut out sod, and set the stones low enough that they won't interfere with mowing.

Wood chips or bark make very satisfactory paths, particularly in woody areas or in gardens where the same material is used as a

◀ *Lay a flagstone walk flush with ground level to make mowing grass easy.*

113

mulch around trees and shrubs. There are some disadvantages: They tend to look messy, they must be rebuilt every two or three years, and they can't be used where the path must be cleared for snow. While wood chips or bark may be expensive at a gardening center, they are often available for little or no money from sawmills or utility companies.

For a *gravel* path, select a local source of supply, since a large volume will be needed. Plan a path two feet wide for single-file traffic and four and a half feet wide for two-abreast traffic. Remove enough topsoil in the path area so that a layer of gravel at least four inches deep can be laid. A layer of cinder can be put down first. A sheet of plastic under the gravel will help to discourage weeds, but because it may also interfere with drainage, it is not recommended.

A gravel walk requires care—removing any weeds, raking smooth several times a year, and at least an annual edging to keep the boundaries straight and specific. Some see the gravel walk as too stiff and formal, but it is excellent for heavy traffic. It is not a good choice for a path that must be kept free of snow.

For the person with an idle chain saw, a tree trunk, and an urge to work, the choice of four- to six-inch *sections of a tree trunk* to be used as stepping stones, is a logical one, but there are reasons to avoid the choice. The sections will need to be treated with a wood preservative (see page 125), they are difficult to place in the ground because of their size and depth, they will be extremely difficult to replace, their appearance tends to deteriorate after a season or two, and they become very slippery, particularly in shaded areas.

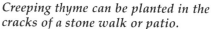

Creeping thyme can be planted in the cracks of a stone walk or patio.

Positive Images, Margaret Hensel

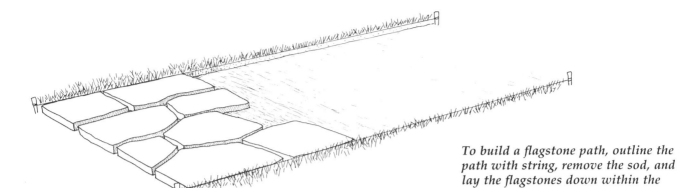

To build a flagstone path, outline the path with string, remove the sod, and lay the flagstones down within the string boundaries.

Flagstone and slate are used in paths in two ways. One way is to set them in concrete, making them the top layer of a concrete walk. The other method, not as good for heavy traffic but far more desirable in every other way, is to place them in the ground, with grass or other plants growing around them.

To build such a path, first outline the path's width with string. Next, remove the sod (use what you remove to renew bare spots in your lawn), and lay down the flagstones within the boundaries of the string. Finally, pack topsoil around the flagstones, and plant grass or plants such as creeping thyme around them. Be sure the stones aren't higher than the lawn level, otherwise they will be a nuisance when they are mowed. Step on each stone to make certain it is solidly planted, so that it won't wiggle when it is walked on.

While grass is perfectly satisfactory around the flagstones, even better is thyme, chamomile, bugleweed, or one of the sedums, all of which grow very well among the stones, adding interest, and sometimes fragrance, to your walk.

Flagstones may be set in a layer of sand three or four inches deep. Be sure this appeals to you before you try it. To some, it has the appearance of islands of stone in a sea of sand.

Bricks laid in sand rather than concrete, are an excellent choice for many situations where a path is needed. They are neat, can be laid in place even by the inexperienced, and require little maintenance. (See pages 116–18 on building a brick walk.)

While new bricks are not inexpensive, often a source of used bricks can be found. They may be less expensive, and at the same time have acquired through age a mottled tone that has a far more pleasing appearance than the sameness of new bricks.

What materials do you prefer for garden paths?

For an average flower garden, grass paths are usually best for two reasons in particular: They present a green foreground for the garden picture, and they need no maintenance other than what the lawn receives. Gravel or flagstone paths in the flower garden are likely to be a nuisance to take care of. Where a path must be dry, or at least passable in all sorts of weather, brick and flagstones are quite serviceable. Often it is possible to make a

The color and texture of a walk made of used bricks adds warmth to this garden, and such a walk is not difficult to construct or maintain.

Maggie Oster

Even as simple a material as pine needles can serve as a garden walk.

grass path more practical and hard-wearing by laying a line of stepping stones down its middle or along one side.

Would you recommend brick or stone edging for a driveway or path?

For a driveway, brick edging is somewhat too fragile unless the bricks are set in a heavy foundation of concrete, which can be unsightly. Try the new plastic driveway edging. It doesn't show, is strong, and is easy to install. For pathways, brick is an ideal edging. Small rounded stones are useless for both driveways and paths, and are not aesthetically pleasing.

I'm planning to lay a brick walk. How do I start?

Begin by determining the answers to the following questions:

- What are the dimensions of your planned walk? First, measure the length. The width should be eighteen to twenty-four inches for one person to walk easily along the path, and four and one-half to five feet for two persons.
- What brick pattern will you use? This is a matter of personal preference. Some patterns, such as herringbone, require cutting the bricks, which means more bricks to buy and lots of brick to be cut. If you have a source of used bricks, they're beautiful for walks.
- What size bricks will you use? You'll find bricks in two sizes, 7 ½-by-3 ½-by-2 ¼ and 8-by-4-by-2 ¾. If you buy bricks, get SW (severe weather) bricks, in the 8-by-4 size.
- How many bricks will you need? If you use 8-by-4 bricks, you'll need four and one-half bricks for each square foot of walk. Plan to edge the walks with bricks set on end horizontally. You will need three per foot, doubled to provide for both sides of the walk.
- How much sand will you need? You will need a two-inch layer of sand under the bricks. Divide the square footage of your walk by six to determine the number of cubic feet of sand you need. Order several buckets extra to fill in the space between bricks.
- Do you have the proper tools? You should have a cart or wheelbarrow, hose, shovel, lawn edger, trowel or some narrow digging tool, tamp, rake, broom, string, hammer, level, and a waste piece of board.

Now that I have my tools, bricks, and sand on the site, what do I do next?

- Your walk should be three-fourths of an inch above the lawn level. The first step is to mark accurately the path boundaries with string. Then remove a six-inch-deep layer of sod and soil within the strings. Use the edger so the edge of your excavation will be straight. (Don't dig out less than this in order to

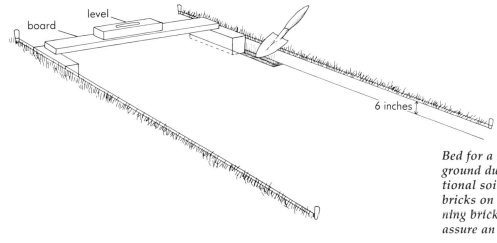

Bed for a new brick walk shows ground dug out 6 inches, with additional soil dug away to lay border bricks on end. A board and level spanning bricks from border to border helps assure an even walk.

avoid using the sand. Without sand, it will be difficult to create a level walk, and drainage on the walk will be poor.)

- Using a trowel, dig out additional space for the upright bricks on each side of the walk, for about three feet of walk. Put the upright bricks in position so that they will be at the level of the walk's surface. Next, use a board and level to span the two lines of bricks, in order to make certain that the lines of bricks are level with each other.
- Shovel a two-inch layer of sand into the walk space, level it, dampen it, and tamp it down. Use a brick to check the depth of the sand layer. Laid flat on the sand, the brick should be the same height as the upright bricks. Taking time to get the sand layer level and the proper depth will make the next steps much easier.
- Set the bricks in position, following your pattern and placing them snugly together for the three-foot section you have edged.
- Make certain all the bricks are level and all are at the same height. Any one that is too high can be lowered by placing a board on it, then hammering the board.
- Continue building short sections, making certain each section is level before moving ahead.
- When all the bricks are in place, scatter sand across the walk, and use a broom to work the sand into the cracks. Hose the walk with a very fine spray, then repeat this step several times to fill all the cracks. After several weeks, and any time you notice space between the bricks, repeat this step.
- As you use the walk, pull up any weeds that push up through the cracks so that they will not have a chance to develop roots that could push the bricks out of position.

I have access to a huge number of bricks from a building that is being demolished, but most of them have mortar clinging to them. Can I get it off?

You're lucky to have that supply of bricks; and yes, the mortar will come off. If they're fairly old, it may come off when you hit

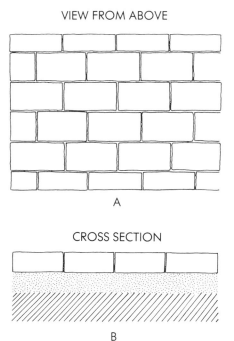

VIEW FROM ABOVE

A

CROSS SECTION

B

(A) Bricks can be laid in many different patterns; the staggered one shown here is quite common, and easy to build; (B) assure adequate drainage by spreading a 2-inch layer of sand over the soil before laying the bricks.

it, gently and at an angle, with a hammer. If this causes you to break a lot of bricks, try soaking them first. Fill a couple of buckets with water and bricks, soak them for a few minutes, and then hammer them again. Be sure to wear safety glasses for this chore; bits of mortar and brick will be flying in all directions.

Used bricks are useful for many purposes, from walks and driveways to construction inside your house. Put aside a good supply of them if you get the chance; you'll be sure to find a use for them.

To build a brick walk with the pattern I like, I must cut some of the bricks. How do I do it?

You'll need a hammer (a heavy bricklayer's hammer is best) and a bricklayer's four-inch chisel.

Tap two bricks together. If each rings, use both. If one gives off a dull sound, it will probably not break true, so don't try to cut it.

Place a brick on a flat, solid surface. With the chisel edge on the line where you want to cut, tip the handle just a bit toward the end of the brick that must be discarded, and hit the brick solidly with the hammer. It should snap through with the first blow. Don't be discouraged if you waste a few bricks before getting the knack. Masons cut bricks so easily that it sometimes discourages the rest of us.

I have a fairly steep path in my yard where I would like to construct steps. Any suggestions?

Do you use the path when pushing a mower or cart or any other heavy equipment? If so, steps can be a real headache and certainly make you sympathize with persons in wheelchairs, who so often find their travels halted by steps and curbs.

Steps can be very effective if the risers (the vertical sections) are no more than eight inches in height and the tread (the horizontal area) is as much as three feet in depth.

A possible combination for this is a railroad tie or some similar timber for the riser, and one of the earlier suggestions for paths

Terraced steps created with railroad-tie risers make an effective and easy-to-maintain walkway on slopes.

for the tread. For example, several flagstones embedded in plantings of thyme would be particularly effective. The sides of these steps offer splendid locations for a collection of shrubs, giving the stroller an excuse to move slowly and enjoy the appearance of both the steps and the shrubs.

Outdoor relaxing and entertaining is infinitely easier and more pleasant if you define a space for such activities. Whether this space takes the form of a patio, terrace, or deck, plan and construct it with care, add comfortable furniture and beautiful plantings, including hanging and other container plants, and your efforts will be rewarded with hours of pleasure.

What is the difference between a patio and a terrace?

In popular thinking, not much, and the terms are used interchangeably. Technically, a terrace is a raised area supported by a wall or bank, while a patio is any paved outdoor living area.

Where should the patio be located?

Immediately outside the living or dining room or the kitchen, where it is easily accessible and can be seen from indoors. Be sure to plan the patio and its plantings so that it is attractive from indoors. The use of sliding glass, French, or patio doors increases the feeling of a connection between inside and outside.

PATIOS

A brick patio, framed by flower beds and furnished with heavy yet airy looking tables and chairs, is an invitation to outdoor living.

Positive Images, Gary Mottau

What is the best material for paving a patio?

You have many choices, depending on your likes and dislikes. The material should go well with the house, particularly with its masonry, such as the foundation and the chimney. Tile, gravel, paving stones, bricks, even redwood planks are all possibilities.

I've been thinking of putting a sandbox for the children on the patio. What do you think?

It's a good idea. Place it at one corner, in the shade, if possible. It provides an excellent place for children to play, and if you place it near a window, you can keep an eye on them while you're in the house. Incorporate it into your design, and after they've outgrown it use it as a planter.

Is there any special furniture that is best for the patio?

It certainly should be weatherproof. Metal chairs and tables that are heavy enough not to be blown around are ideal. Lounging chairs should be of a style that complements the architecture of both the house and the patio.

I would like to have some flower beds on my patio. Do they belong?

They certainly do. You might consider building raised beds using sides of brick or stone to make the planting surface about two feet above the ground. Herbs planted in such beds are more readily smelled and touched, and weeding is not as backbreaking as in ground-level beds.

FENCES AND WALLS, NATURAL AND MANMADE

Consider these two rules before building fences.

- Decide exactly why you need the fence, then select a fence that will harmonize with the surroundings and be the least obtrusive, yet still do the job.
- Make certain you have a legal right to erect a fence. Do you know the exact location of your property boundary? You can be in trouble if you erect a fence slightly over that line. Does your community have zoning laws on fences? Some towns prohibit tall fences; others have different restrictions. Does your deed prohibit the erection of any types of fences? Some do, and were written in to protect the open look of a neighborhood that has no fences.

Your choice of fencing materials is vast. There are a great many plants that are probably better than building materials for most home use. Here are some of them:

Trees are particularly good for blocking views and acting as wind breaks. Be sure to consider the mature size of a tree before selecting it. Some trees, such as spruce and hemlock, can be

Positive Images, Jerry Howard

Artfully placed evergreen shrubs inter-planted with deciduous flowering shrubs and trees form a screen to dis-guise the lattice fence along the property line in this yard. The fore-ground is further enhanced by a stone retaining wall and ground covers.

planted in a row to form a high hedge that is virtually impreg-nable, is easy to care for, and offers a beauty and grace not found in a carefully clipped hedge.

Shrubs can be used to form either deciduous or evergreen hedges up to fifteen feet high. Formally clip them or allow them to reach their natural form guided only by occasional prunings.

Among the broad-leaved evergreens useful for hedges are crape myrtle, boxwood, privet, pyrocantha, and rhododendron. Juniper, yew, and blue spruce are only three of the many coniferous shrubs that will provide both beauty and a barrier.

Deciduous shrubs such as quince, forsythia, lilac, elderberry, and hydrangea often grow thickly enough so that a hedge of them makes a formidable barrier even when they have shed their leaves. Many of these are excellent if you need only to suggest a wall, such as near a patio. For such use, give them enough space so each plant reaches its full size and beauty.

Vines have the advantage of providing a barrier without using a great deal of space. Trees and shrubs use a band of space six or more feet in width, while a vine growing on a fence will thrive in a space only a foot wide. At the same time, it will easily reach as high as a two-story building, if that is wanted. Vines, too, are invaluable for hiding the fortresslike features of walls and

Simple

Drooping wisteria blossoms soften the harshness of a high brick wall.

heavy-duty fences, if allowed to cover heavily enough to appear to be a hedge.

Vines are extremely versatile. Some make excellent ground covers, some cling to walls, some have thorns to emphasize their roles as walls to halt traffic, and many of them are fragrant. Some vines, including clematis and English ivy, are fine for covering and hiding walls or even rock outcroppings. Wisteria, climbing hydrangea, and Virginia creeper will cling to walls. The climbing rose, jasmine, and clematis all offer beautiful blossoms. Select vines that will grow in your climate and that are fitted for the job you want done.

Screens, available in many colors, sizes, and materials, are excellent for temporary walls. They are easy to put up and to store.

Fences range from electric and barbed wire (neither of which should be used where there is human—and particularly juvenile—traffic) to solid sections of wood. They serve many functions, blocking views, supporting vines, protecting areas from unwelcome winds, and keeping animals in or out.

Fencing must be selected to fit with your landscaping and the style of your house. Think for a moment about where a picket or post-and-rail fence would look best, and you will understand the need for a careful choice. The split-rail fence is excellent around many gardens and will support vines. It looks particularly good under a healthy growth of climbing roses in country settings. The wood hurdle fence is another choice for that setting. Woven-paling fences can be chosen for complete privacy or as a background for a garden.

Vertical board fences, too, can offer complete privacy. They're built with six- or eight-inch boards nailed to two two-by-four rails that are supported with posts. Louvered fences are similar in construction, but the boards are set at an angle so they do not interfere with the flow of air.

Wire fences range from chain-link fences to lighter wires. They are utilitarian and are best if disguised by a heavy vine.

I want to grow a high hedge around three sides of our lot. My husband opposes this. What do you think?

In "Mending Wall," poet Robert Frost answered this best. Frost said that before he built a wall (and your high hedge would be a wall) he would like to know what he was walling in or walling out. The hedge you suggest could be valuable for blocking a view of some eyesore, such as a used car lot. It might serve as a background for flower beds, and it can be a good windbreak in winter. But remember that it will make a narrow lot look narrower, and a small lot appear smaller. In addition, it will destroy your views on three sides. No longer can you and your neighbors share a sense of spaciousness, allowing all of you to share your lawns and trees visually.

Would a mixture of plants with variously colored leaves or blossoms be satisfactory for informal screening to enclose a yard?

Yes, if you plant them in groups of five, seven, or nine, depending on the length of the border. Accent the groups of shrubs at intervals with taller evergreens or flowering trees. This type of border takes up more room than hedges.

What is the best fence for use along the road in front of a modified colonial house where something elaborate would be inappropriate?

A simple post-and-rail fence has long proved very satisfactory in such situations. It can be painted white, or, if made of cypress or redwood, left unpainted to weather. If it is meant to keep out (or in) small animals, chicken wire can be attached to the inside at the bottom and disguised by plants.

Is a wattle fence appropriate for the home garden?

Yes, it is excellent for screening a small garden utility area, and it provides privacy. Wattle fences are made of thin split saplings and are quite durable.

Do you recommend wire gates for gardens?

Wire gates are suitable for vegetable areas or dog runs, but for other purposes, something more decorative, such as a wooden or iron gate, should be chosen.

The profusion of blooms of a climbing rose makes it the ideal companion for a split-rail fence.

Positive Images, Jerry Howard

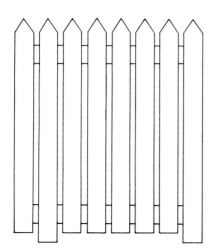
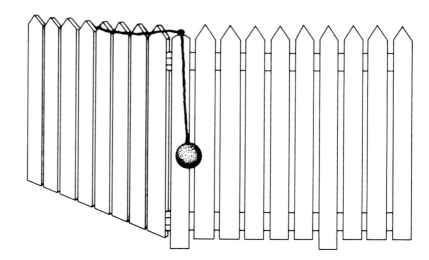

A colonial gate fixture is a practical way to be certain gates are closed, even today. The heavy ball drops down and pulls the gate closed.

We have a picket fence gate that visitors invariably leave open. How do you construct one that is self-closing?

The method used in colonial times still works well. Attach a heavy ball to a chain. On the hinged side of the gate, put a post to the side so the gate opens away from it. Attach one end of the chain to the top of the post, the other to the top of the gate, and have enough slack in the chain so that it is tight only when the gate is fully open. In this way, the weight of the ball will close the open gate.

I'd like to build a stone retaining wall. Do you think this is too difficult for an amateur to undertake?

On a sloping lot, a retaining wall can both serve many functions as well as add beauty to the property. A wall built as explained below will be stable to a height of four feet. For higher walls, you may wish to employ a contractor. Check your local ordinances; sometimes building permits are required for retaining walls. Here are some rules that will make construction easier:

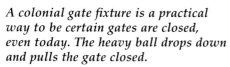
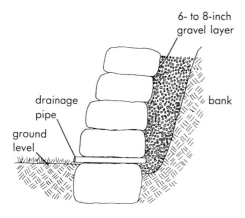

- Dig out a space so the first tier of stones will be below ground level and provide a firm foundation for the wall.
- Just above ground level, place several one-inch diameter pipes (one every six to eight feet) through the wall; they should be as long as the width of the wall.
- Place a six- to eight-inch-wide layer of gravel or crushed stone behind the entire wall, adding the gravel as you add layers of stones to the wall. This layer plus the pipes will prevent a buildup of water behind the wall.
- Keep the wall leaning slightly toward the bank, about three inches per foot height of the wall. Lay the individual stones flat; do not lean them against the bank.
- Place each stone so that it is resting on two or more below it.
- If long stones are available, place them so they anchor the wall into the bank.

Cross-section of a stone retaining wall, showing large foundation stone below ground level, drainage pipe through wall just above ground level, 6- to 8-inch wide layer of gravel behind entire wall, wall leaning toward bank, and stones laid flat with largest stones at the bottom.

- Place the largest stones at the bottom of the wall.
- If flat stones are available, save them to use as a cap for the wall.

Some of my fencing is not pressure-treated; should I apply a preservative?

As you landscape your property, you'll want to use wood preservatives in order to protect wood used for fence posts or in the construction of lawn steps, terraces, and furniture. Following a few rules will make this a safer venture.

- Avoid the use of creosote. It's highly poisonous and will kill any plants that come in contact with it. Most railroad ties have been creosoted. Old ties that have weathered for years, however, are safe to use in most conditions.
- In situations where wood will be buried, such as fence posts, buy pressure-treated wood. It will last years longer than wood you treat yourself.
- When buying a preservative, read the label first. It will tell you what fungicide is used, whether it protects against termites, whether it can be painted over, and whether it should be used where the wood will be in contact with the soil.

Are wood preservatives dangerous to handle?

Today a growing number of wood preservatives are being developed that offer long-lasting protection against rotting and that are at the same time not dangerous to use and not harmful to persons or plant life. Some of the less dangerous preservatives contain copper naphthenate, copper-8-quinolinolate, polyphase, or TBTO. Even though these preservatives are much safer to use than some of the older ones that are no longer manufactured, they should still be handled with care. Wear goggles, long sleeves, gloves, and a dust mask while applying, and don't handle the wood while it is still damp with preservatives. Here are a few guidelines:

- Work in the shade. That way the preservative will penetrate the wood before drying.
- Work on clean wood. If it's dirty, scrub it, then allow it to dry. This can take several days.
- Don't try to treat painted wood. It will do no good.
- If possible, dip the wood into the preservative, rather than painting it on. This permits the preservative to get into small cracks in the wood that a brush will skim over.
- Keep an eye on the wood after you have treated it. If it is constantly damp after treatment because of poor drainage, it will rot much more quickly. If you see mildew on it, scrub it with a mixture of bleach and water, and let the wood dry for several days; then treat it with preservative again. Plan on applying preservative again to all wood after two or three days.

A stone retaining wall of substantial flat rocks is a handsome and serviceable addition to this property.

6 *Special Gardens*

This final chapter is a selection of garden types, some or all of which you may wish to incorporate into your landscape design. In each case, we give you only an introduction, with the hope that your appetite will be whetted for more adventures into the fascinating worlds of growing vegetables and herbs, planning specialty gardens such as rock gardens or gardens for the handicapped and elderly, and sharing your delight in gardening with children and even the birds that will find your landscape an inviting and secure haven for feeding and nesting. Happy gardening!

KITCHEN GARDENS

Vegetable gardens intended simply to supply a single family's table with fresh, crisp, and succulent vegetables are often referred to as kitchen gardens. And who says such a garden can look only functional? Carefully planned and tended, it can be an important decorative feature of your landscape at the same time it provides you food. For the beginner, a vegetable garden no more than ten by ten feet is a good starting size. Follow the principles described on pages 105–11 for soil preparation.

Decorative kitchen gardens demand that you first put aside outmoded ideas of what a vegetable garden should look like: Rather than lining crops up in single file, plant them in beds a foot or more wide. For example, start lettuce plants no more than two inches apart on all sides. Then, as the lettuce grows, keep thinning (and eating) it, so that it will have ample room even when it is full grown. Carrots, too, can be grown this way,

◆ *The hollowed center of the large rock forms a perfect bird bath in the midst of this herb and flower garden.*

Vegetable gardens need not be merely utilitarian. A creative design using raised beds makes this one a center-piece of the landscape. Paths are mulched with salt marsh hay.

about two inches apart, and their feathery foliage will make a delightful blanket.

What vegetables, in addition to lettuce and carrots, are good for beginning gardeners with limited space?

Include a few of the smaller tomato plants, such as Pixie or the even smaller bush cherry tomatoes. Nothing is more decorative than pepper plants, with their shiny green foliage, and their heavy harvest provides an added incentive to grow them. Cucumbers take up space, running their vines here and there, but if you must be miserly with space, grow these on a fence or on trellis netting. Alternatively, select the bush varieties and get ample rewards even from small spaces. Broccoli has recently been widely promoted for its health benefits and deserves a space in the smallest gardens. Each plant bears one large head, followed after the main harvest by bite-sized sprouts all summer. Only such space-eaters as corn and potatoes must be excluded from the small garden.

How can I get the most out of my limited space?

Keep the soil producing: For example, have at least six plantings of various kinds of lettuce, starting one crop in a flat as another is reaching maturity. Don't waste an inch of space. If you have a small empty spot, plant another crop of radishes or a few onions that can be harvested at any time for salads.

I keep reading about growing lettuce all summer long. I try it, and it becomes so bitter it is not worth eating. Any suggestions?

Try varieties such as Oak Leaf, Salad Bowl, and Buttercrunch to find the one that does best in the summer weather in your region. Try growing lettuce in the shade: for example, on the north side of tall plants such as tomatoes, or under something that will give partial shade, such as several layers of cheesecloth. Finally, keep it moist at all times.

If none of these suggestions succeeds, don't give up. In midsummer during the hottest days, start a flat of lettuce indoors. It will be up and ready to be transplanted into the garden in mid-August for a fine fall crop.

I've tried planting beets in beds and find they are too crowded before reaching maturity. Am I planting them too closely together?

No, but you are missing one of the best ways to eat beets. When the plants begin to get crowded, thin them to give those remaining the space they need. Cook the thinnings, roots and all, as greens. Many people grow beets just for this, preferring the greens to the mature beets.

What vegetables can be grown in beds?

Just about any of them: It's simply a matter of leaving enough space between plants so they will thrive. For instance, beets, carrots, leaf lettuce, onions, and radishes should be planted only two to three inches apart; cabbages, cauliflower, and peppers should be a foot apart; and tomatoes should be two to three feet apart. Pole beans are one crop that does best in a single row. For best pollination, corn should be in several rows, rather than one long, single row.

I want to make several raised beds by framing them with six-by-six timbers. The wood won't last long unless it is treated. What do you suggest?

Your best choice is factory pressure-treated wood, which will last for many years. If you wish to try to do it yourself, select a copper naphthenate preservative. Cuprinol green #10 is one of these, and there are others. Treatment should make the wood last several years. It will last even longer if you take the trouble to pull up the timbers, brush the soil off them each fall, and treat them with preservative again every two or three years. This preservative will not harm the plants in your beds. (See page 125 for precautions to take in handling wood preservatives.)

HERB GARDENS

An herb garden can be as modest as a clump or two of chives beside the kitchen door, or as extravagant as the English knot gardens that entwine many herbs in beguiling patterns. It can be purely decorative—as those English gardens certainly are—or it can be grown for culinary purposes or even for medicinal use. It can be a garden for those herbs you use daily—parsley, mint, dill, and basil, perhaps—or it can be a place to try new herbs, such as chervil or hyssop, borage or lovage. An herb garden can be exactly what you want it to be. Keep it close by your kitchen door, as has been custom since prehistoric days when it was discovered easier to grow these cherished plants close to the cave entrance, rather than to seek them out when the need arose.

I'd like to grow herbs, but I don't know where to begin.

Before herbs grow best for us, as with other plants we must understand their likes and dislikes about sunlight and shade, moisture, and richness of soil. Some are annuals, some are the most persistent of perennials, and a few, like caraway and parsley, are biennials.

If you wish to try growing herbs but hesitate, fearing failure, begin with a very small area. Spade up a square, three-feet-by-three-feet, in a sunny spot with reasonably good soil. Or make a raised bed by nailing together a three-foot-by-three-foot square of two-by-six-inch boards, then filling it with soil.

What herbs grow most successfully?

Plant those herbs you now use and like. Chives are perennials, easy to start, and hard to discourage. They demand only that you clip them occasionally (clip the entire stem when you harvest them). Parsley is slow to start, but very prolific when it's underway. Dill is excellent, particularly if you pickle cucumbers. Mint is an old standby, but be ready for it to try to take over your garden. Basil is wonderful in tomato dishes. Try as well a few herbs with which you are not as familiar. Tall lovage is useful in many dishes. Borage has a taste much like cucumbers. In your small bed, you can try as many as nine herbs, allotting a square foot to each one.

A year or two with this tiny garden and you will be ready for more ambitious undertakings. Medicinal plants? An intertwining of herbs that will astonish your visitors? Herbs for tea? The choice is yours.

I've raised parsley and know it is a biennial plant, yet I have never had it reappear in the spring. Why not?

You're right, parsley is a biennial, which means it produces its seeds the second year. It does not mean that it is winter hardy. People raising parsley in cold climates should harvest the leaves the first year and plant another crop the next year.

Neat and formal, this herb garden thrives in the sandy soil and bright sun of the seashore.

Positive Images, Jerry Howard

I would like to put herb plants around the spokes of an old wagon wheel. How would you suggest doing this?

It can be made into the central feature of a small, formal herb garden. Select a level, sunny spot in the garden, and prepare the soil as you would for any garden. Put the wheel down, then plant a different variety of herbs between each set of spokes. So that the spokes won't be hidden, we would suggest using fairly small plants such as thyme, chives, sage, parsley, mint, French tarragon, winter savory, sweet basil, and chervil.

When should herbs be harvested?

By all means, harvest them as you need them. Select a few each evening for the dinner salad, and marvel at the difference. Try them in cooking. If you wish to save them for winter use, however, harvest them before they flower. Cut them early in the morning, wash them, then dry them with circulating air, not heat. When they are thoroughly dry, strip the leaves off the twigs and store the leaves in airtight containers.

ROCK GARDENS

There are rock gardens—and there are piles of rocks with plants growing among them. The difference is that the developers of the *gardens* studied and pondered, viewed and compared before making a move.

The sites of rock gardens vary widely. Often they are on problem slopes where grass would not grow well. Converted to a rock garden, such a place becomes a plus in the landscaping. Rock gardens can also be level areas, with added soil and rocks creating a setting for a collection of plants. They can even be rocky outcroppings, where the natural setting is changed only by the addition of plants.

Often they are shaded, but some are in sunny areas, and some of the best combine shaded and sunny areas, providing a variety of conditions for a variety of plants.

Can you give some general guidelines for a successful rock garden?

- Feature large plants only if the garden is large. Some of the most effective gardens are small, with everything in them—rocks and all plants—small and thus not dominating the space.
- Rock gardens are not rock collections. Use only one type of stone, usually native stone, which is cheaper and more suitable for the area. Quarried rock, such as blocks of marble, should be avoided as it detracts from the natural look of the garden.
- Place rocks naturally, partially buried, so that they look as if they belonged there and were not just placed there. Avoid round stones, particularly those sitting on top of the ground.

Gaily flowering, low-growing plants are perfect foils for the rough, light colored stones. Shrubs such as the cotoneaster spreading over the large rock on the left further soften the setting.

- Place plants so that you can easily reach them when you garden. This is not a garden you can plant and forget. Although the best gardens have a natural look, as if they somehow created themselves, this appearance is deceptive. Like any other gardens, these must be cared for—weeded, divided, cut back, fertilized, and sometimes watered.

- Feature plants indigenous to the area. In years past, many rock gardens featured the small alpine plants that flourish in cool, rocky areas. But while these plants are still popular in northern areas, you are not limited to them. Beautiful rock gardens can be found in desert areas, as well as in the warm and humid conditions of the Deep South, each with plants appropriate to the climate and topography.

- Most rock gardens feature perennials that grow close to the ground, and particularly those that grow over and cling to the rocks.

- Start small. Create a small gem of a garden, and then gradually enlarge it.

- Some rock gardens have the added beauty of running water, a tiny falls, perhaps, or water running across rocks and into a pool. Any such use of water will enhance the beauty of the garden and attract birds to the site. If there is no natural water on the site, a falls or stream can be created, using a recirculating pump.

Where can I get more information about rock gardens?

Visit the gardens of friends (or even strangers, who usually are happy to display their gardens, if asked politely), or visit the rockeries of botanical gardens, where the plants usually are identified with small signs. This provides an opportunity to identify and select plants you wish for your own garden.

The list of plants ideal for a rock garden is long. Most garden centers stock plants that are suitable for rock gardens in their area. In general, these are low-growing plants, modest when blossoming, some with green or silver foliage, some evergreen. In most gardens, it is most effective to plant in groups, rather than scatter various plants across the garden.

Are there plants I should avoid putting in my rock garden?

There are some plants that do not belong in a rock garden because they tend to overwhelm its subtle beauty. The bold blooms of zinnias and marigolds, for example, tend to over-shadow smaller plants. Some evergreens blend well in a rock garden, but those commonly found around house foundations will look overdressed and out of place. Large plants can be used, but very carefully. They are possibly best as background for the smaller plants.

How much of a rock garden should be covered with rocks?

There is no rule for this. In general, on flat areas or gentle slopes, allow broad spaces between rocks. On steeper slopes, many more rocks look very natural. In any case, large rocks look better than small.

I have access to a lot of big stone blocks that will split much like slate. Is this appropriate for a rock garden?

I am assuming these are rough blocks, not square-cut in a quarry. If so, they are excellent. But use them carefully. Thin pieces, such as slates, will look out of place. And when you position those blocks, their layers of stratification (the lines along which you could split them) should all run the same way, slightly off from horizontal.

How deep should rock plants be set in the ground?

Most form a spreading top that either roots as it spreads or grows directly from a central root system. The crown of the plant must not be covered. Dig a hole with a trowel and gather the loose tops in your hand. Holding the plant at the side of the hole with the crown resting on the surface and the roots extending into the hole, firm the soil around the roots. When the hole is filled, the crown should rest on the surface. Give it a good watering to establish it.

My rock garden site is a natural one, with lots of outcroppings and little topsoil. Any suggestions?

You have a good setting for a rock garden. For best results, look for places where you can dig out pockets among the stones to fill with topsoil to give your plants a better chance for success. If your site is sunny, these plants may require watering during dry spells, long before you think of watering your lawn or flower beds.

When is the best time to plant a rock garden?

If pot-grown plants are available, planting may be done almost any time from spring to early autumn. Although spring is good everywhere, September and October work well in moderately cold climates, such as lower New York State.

A GARDEN FOR THE ELDERLY OR HANDICAPPED

This raised garden in a housing project for the elderly offers easy access for gardeners in wheelchairs or those for whom kneeling is difficult.

Positive Images, Jerry Howard

For elderly and handicapped people, life often becomes a saddening sequence of giving up beloved activities. Gardening need not be among these, and the stronger gardeners among us can make certain that it isn't. The degree of assistance required depends on the person involved.

I know an elderly couple both of whom have always loved to garden, but who now feel they must give it up because they can no longer operate their 100-by-100-foot garden. Bending over, weeding and harvesting—it's just too much. Any suggestions?

If a volunteer gardener creates a raised bed for them, narrow enough so they can reach to the center of it, long enough to grow their needs, they can continue gardening. There's less bending with the raised bed, making wide rows of lettuce, carrots, or beans easy to care for and harvest.

How can more handicapped persons, perhaps even those confined to wheelchairs, be enabled to garden?

A garden on legs offers dramatic possibilities for raising flowers or vegetables. This can be a table-like creation, on sturdy legs and with wooden sides to hold six inches of soil.

Can container gardening be done successfully by those unable to manage larger-scale gardens?

Container gardening can indeed bring to elderly and severely handicapped persons the deep satisfaction that more ambitious gardening offers. Container gardening can mean many things: a window box on a patio, easily cultivated from a chair and offering as much as six square feet of gardening space, or just a few clay pots with favorite geraniums in them.

Pot up a Pixie tomato plant in a large pot and present it to a person who thinks his or her gardening days are over. Place the plant in a sunny spot, handy for the person who will tend it, stake it up with a light stick, and provide a liquid fertilizer for occasional use. That tomato plant will receive the tenderest of TLC, bring interest to what may be a drab life, and contribute a golfball-size tomato or more per day all summer long. See this happen once and you'll be convinced of the therapeutic value of raising plants.

My father suffers from arthritis so that holding a tool such as a hoe is painful. Any suggestions?

For some people, the pain results from closing the hands tightly enough to hold the tool. Try padding the handle with several layers of cloth so his hands do not have to close tightly to hold the tool. This is particularly useful for many persons attempting to handle small tools such as trowels.

Once upon a time, there were two children. The first child was introduced to gardening at the age of eight. His father and mother planted the garden, and then when weeds began to compete with lettuce, carrots, and *their* interest in gardening, the weeding was assigned to him. And he did it for five years, weeding, weeding, weeding—and grumbling, grumbling,

CHILDREN'S GARDENS

•

Quick-growing lettuce is a good choice for young gardeners.

Positive Images, Jerry Howard

It's never too soon to introduce children to the wonder of watching tiny seeds spring into showy flowers or tasty vegetables.

grumbling. He hasn't gardened since, nor, thankfully has he passed the work on to his next generation.

The second child began gardening at the age of six. She saw her parents in the garden, thought it looked like fun, asked for a garden of her own, and was assigned her own small space. She even got to choose her crops—pansies and radishes. She learned much that summer: how pansies can be picked and picked and still keep producing; how radishes, if planted every week, will be ready to pick every night for dinner, even when parents suggest saving some for dinner the following night. The next summer she learned how far pumpkin vines will run. And the next—was it the year of the six varieties of tomatoes, or the one of the giant sunflowers that nodded in friendly fashion to all who entered the garden?

The moral of the story is not difficult to understand. Gardening should be fun, not a chore, for youngsters. They should raise what they want to, even if raising twelve corn plants seems unproductive. Their achievements should be applauded, their failures handled constructively as lessons in horticulture—or even ignored. And if the six-year-old's interest in gardening cools in the heat of early July, that should not be recalled when he or she wants to try again the next spring.

What are good plants for children to begin with?

Children like things to happen quickly and plainly. For this reason, radishes, which seem to pop out of the soil in a matter of days, are a good choice. The growth of pole beans running up a pole can be tracked daily. A mixture of annual flowers adds a mystery to the garden: What's that, a weed or a flower?

A GARDEN FOR BIRDS

It's possible, and quite simple, to create a haven for birds as you landscape your yard. On large properties, this can mean providing food, water, cover, and places for nesting. If your land area is more modest, it can mean a few dogwoods or other shrubs that provide food that birds especially love.

How can I encourage birds to come to our yard?

Remember that birds like a variety of conditions, such as open lawn areas, the cover of shrubs and trees, small flowering trees, and pools or bird baths in which to bathe. They also love conditions that aren't too tidy, such as thick growths of brambles, brush piles, heavy growths around fences, and fallen trees.

Birdhouses, too, will encourage birds to your property. Consult a chart that shows sizes of homes and entrance sizes and heights of homes for various birds. Don't bother with perches at the entrance. They aren't needed, and provide roosts for other birds to heckle the inhabitants.

How can I protect birds from cats?

Cats are the worst enemy of birds. Remember this as you plan your bird garden, and put baths and feeding stations away from shrubs, so cats can't sneak up on the birds.

Can I choose specific plants that birds enjoy in order to make our yard more inviting?

Berry bushes, Virginia creeper, and dogwoods will all attract birds during the summer. Several attractive shrubs have the added virtue of carrying their fruits into the winter, and thus providing food for the birds. These include barberries, cotoneasters, hawthorns, holly, mountain ash, roses, snowberries, and viburnum. Add to what is offered naturally by providing food such as suet, wheat, hemp, sunflower seeds, millet, and raisins.

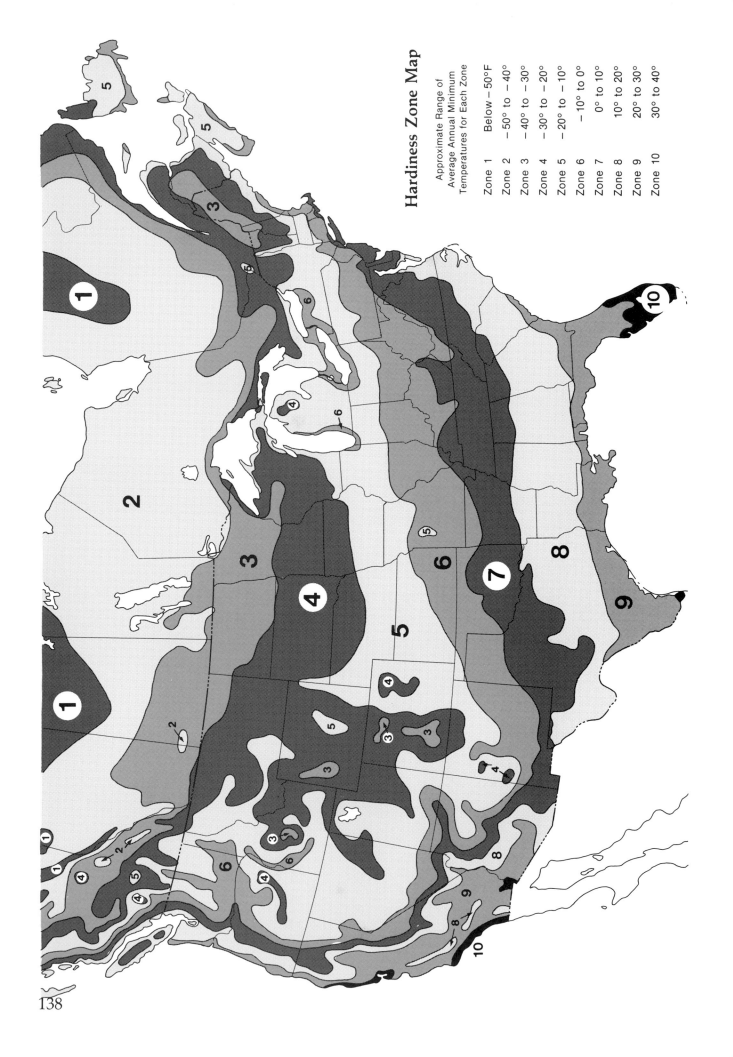

Hardiness Zone Map

Approximate Range of
Average Annual Minimum
Temperatures for Each Zone

Zone 1   Below −50°F
Zone 2   −50° to −40°
Zone 3   −40° to −30°
Zone 4   −30° to −20°
Zone 5   −20° to −10°
Zone 6   −10° to 0°
Zone 7   0° to 10°
Zone 8   10° to 20°
Zone 9   20° to 30°
Zone 10   30° to 40°

Glossary

ACID SOIL. See pH.

ALKALINE SOIL. See pH.

ANNUAL. A plant that is raised from seed, flowers, fruits, and dies within one season.

BALLED-AND-BURLAPPED PLANTS. Plants that have been dug carefully with the soil around their roots maintained, wrapped in burlap, and tied.

BARE-ROOTED PLANTS. A plant without soil attached to its roots.

BIENNIAL. A plant that takes two years to complete its growing cycle from seed; usually flowers, fruits, and dies during its second season.

BORDER. A bed of flowers along a walk, fence, property line, or building.

BULB. The fleshy root of plants such as tulips and daffodils; a bulb stores the roots, stems, leaves, and flowers for the next season's growth.

CLAY SOIL. A soil containing from thirty- to 100-percent clay; fine-textured and sticky when wet.

COMPOST. A rich, porous soil of completely decayed organic matter.

CORM. A modified stem filled with food storage tissue; a fleshy root similar to a bulb, but not solid.

CULTIVAR. A plant variety, usually unique and an improvement in the species.

DEADHEADING. Cutting off flower heads after they bloom.

DECIDUOUS PLANTS. A plant that sheds most or all of its leaves yearly; not evergreen.

DIVISION. A method of plant propagation in which plants (including their root system) are dug and cut apart; the resulting plants can all be replanted.

EVERGREEN. A plant whose foliage stays green and functional through more than one growing season.

EXTENSION SERVICE. This agency is the educational arm of the U.S. Federal Department of Agriculture. There is a branch in every county in the country, often affiliated with the state university.

FOUNDATION PLANTINGS. Deciduous and evergreen shrubs planted along the foundation of a house.

FUNGICIDE. A formulation that destroys or inhibits the growth of fungi.

GERMINATION. The sprouting of seeds.

GRADE. A slope's degree of incline. Adequate drainage is provided by a drop of one foot for every thirty feet of surface.

GREEN MANURE. A cover crop, such as crimson clover and hairy vetch in the South and rye, winter rye, buckwheat, and field peas in the North, that is tilled under when it grows about one foot high, and that decomposes, thus providing natural fertilizer for lawns and gardens.

GROUND COVER. Low-growing plants that cover the ground instead of lawn grass.

GUY WIRE. A wire used to brace or support.

HERBICIDE. A formulation used to inhibit or destroy plant growth; some are developed to affect only specific kinds of plants.

INSECTICIDE. A formulation that destroys insects.

LAWN. An overcrowded population of several varieties of dwarf grass plants.

LEACHING. A process in which water percolates through the soil, washing out soluble matter.

LEADER. The primary shoot of a plant.

LOAM. A soil consisting of about a 50-50 mixture of sand and clay; a ball of damp loam will not break when handled.

MULCH. A protective covering, such as bark chips or sawdust, spread over the ground to reduce evaporation, maintain an even soil temperature, prevent erosion, control weeds, and enrich the soil.

NITROGEN. One of the three most important plant nutrients, an essential element of chlorophyll; stunted growth and pale yellow foliage indicate nitrogen deficiency. See also Potassium, Phosphorus.

NPK. Numbers representing the proportion of nitrogen, phosphorus, and potassium, respectively, in chemical fertilizers.

NURSE GRASS. In seed mixtures, a grass variety that comes up first until the slower starting, permanent turf can take over.

PEAT MOSS. Compacted plant debris, including sphagnum moss.

PERENNIAL. A plant with a life cycle of three or more seasons.

PESTICIDE. An all-embracing term for any agent that is used to destroy pests.

PH. The relative acidity and alkalinity of a soil on a scale of 1 to 14; a soil with a pH of 7 is considered neutral.

PHOSPHORUS. One of the three most important plant nutrients, essential for good root and stem development; stunted growth and purple coloring of leaves and stems indicate phosphorus deficiency. See also Nitrogen, Potassium.

PITCH. See Grade.

PLUG. A small cube or biscuit of sod about two inches wide and two inches deep.

POSTEMERGENT HERBICIDE. A formulation that destroys only seedlings or growing plants, not germinating seeds.

POTASSIUM. One of the three most important plant nutrients; slow growth, high incidence of disease, and bronzing of leaves indicate potassium deficiency. See also Nitrogen, Phosphorus.

PREEMERGENT HERBICIDE. A formulation that destroys *only* germinating seeds, not seedlings.

PROPAGATION. A way of multiplying plants.

RHIZOME. An underground, horizontal stem or root stock.

ROTOTILL. To operate a rotary tiller.

SANDY SOIL. A soil with from fifty- to 100-percent fine sands, as well as coarse sands with thirty-five- to 100-percent fine gravel and some fine sand. Although sandy soil can be formed into a ball when wet, the ball will break easily when touched.

SLOW-RELEASE FERTILIZERS. Fertilizers specially formulated to release their active ingredients over a long period of time.

SOD. Rolls or squares of mature grass, cut out of the ground with about one inch of roots and soil attached, for placement on a prepared bed.

SOIL AMENDMENTS. Ingredients such as sand, peat moss, or compost that are added to soil to improve its texture.

SOIL TEST. A measurement of the nitrogen/phosphorus/potassium and pH levels of the soil. Gardeners can test their own soil with soil testing kits, or send soil samples to Extension Services.

SPRIG. A stem fragment with young blades of grass and bits of root attached.

STOLON. A shoot that takes root as it runs along the surface of the ground.

SUBGRADE. The surface that serves as the foundation for the finished grade, or topsoil.

SUPERPHOSPHATE. A soluble mixture of phosphates used as a fertilizer; made by treating insoluble phosphates with sulfuric acid.

THATCH. A layer of dead grass and leaves that builds up between the soil and the grass blades and cuts off the flow of moisture to the grass roots.

TILLING. Working the soil by cultivating or digging it.

TIP CUTTINGS. A method of plant propagation in which three to six inches is cut from the top of a plant and planted in potting mix until the cutting puts forth roots.

TOPDRESSING. A rich mixture of soil and organic matter to scatter as fertilizer over the surface.

TOPSOIL. The surface layer of soil, consisting of good loam and organic matter.

TRANSPIRATION. A process by which plants lose their moisture, usually through their leaves.

VERMICULITE. Lightweight, highly water-absorbent material resulting from the expansion of mica granules under high temperatures, used as a potting medium.

Books for Further Reading

Agricultural Chemicals, W.T. Thomson, Thomson Publications

All About Landscaping, Lin Cotton, Chevron Chemical Co.

American Gardens: A Traveler's Guide, Brooklyn Botanic Garden

The Bug Book, John and Helen Philbrick, Storey Communications, Inc./ Garden Way Publishing

The Complete Book of Edible Landscaping, Rosalind Creasy, Sierra Club Books

Crockett's Flower Garden, James Underwood Crockett, Little, Brown, and Co.

Diseases of Trees and Shrubs, Wayne A. Sinclair, Howard H. Lyon, and Warren T. Johnson, Comstock Publishing Association

The Education of A Gardener, Russell Page, Random House

For Every Home a Garden, Rudy and Joy Favretti, The Pequot Press

The Garden Border Book, Mary Keen, Capability's Books

A Garden for Your Birds, Rupert Barrrington, Grosset and Dunlap

The Gardener's Guide to Better Soil, Gene Logsdon, Rodale Press

Ground Cover Plants, Donald Wyman, The Macmillan Company

Handbook on Biological Control of Plant Pests, Brooklyn Botanic Garden

Lawns, Brooklyn Botanic Garden

Lawns and Ground Covers, Sunset Books and Sunset Magazine editors, Name Publishing Co.

The Nature of Landscape Design, Nan Fairbrother, Alfred A. Knopf

Nature's Design, Carol A. Symser and the editors of Rodale Press, Rodale Press, 1982

The New American Landscape Gardener: A Guide to Beautiful Backyards and Sensational Surroundings, Phebe Leighton and Calvin Simonds, Rodale Press

The Organic Gardener, Catharine Osgood Foster, Alfred A. Knopf

Plants in Action, Judy Brooks and Ron Bloomfield, editors, British Broadcasting Corp.

Pruning Simplified, Lewis Hill, Storey Communications/Garden Way Publishing

Secrets of Plant Propagation, Lewis Hill, Storey Communications/Garden Way Publishing

The Shrub Identification Book, George W.D. Symonds, William Morrow & Co.

Site Planning Standards, Joseph Chiara, McGraw-Hill Book Co.

Taylor's Encyclopedia of Gardening, Norman Taylor, editor, Houghton Mifflin

Theme Gardens, Barbara Damrosch, Workman Publishing

Index

145